Oil & Vinegar

An emulsion of recipes from the
Junior League of Tulsa, Inc.

Oil & Vinegar

An emulsion of recipes from the
Junior League of Tulsa, Inc.

Oil & Vinegar

Published by the Junior League of Tulsa, Inc.
3633 South Yale Avenue
Tulsa, Oklahoma
918-663-6100
www.jltulsa.org

Edited, designed, and manufactured in the
United States of America by
Favorite Recipes® Press
an imprint of

FRP

2451 Atrium Way
Nashville, Tennessee 37214

Production Director: Mark Sloan
Managing Editor: Mary Cummings
Art Director: Steve Newman
Book Design: Brad Whitfield
Production Design: Susan Breining
Project Manager: Jane Hinshaw
Project Administrator: Tanis Westbrook
Project Production: Sara Anglin

Library of Congress Number: 2001 135017
ISBN: 0-9604368-0-4
First Printing: 2002   20,000 copies

Cover artist Otto Duecker is a nationally
recognized artist who resides in Tulsa. He has
been a professional artist for more than
twenty-five years and shows his work in New
York, Scottsdale, Birmingham, MI, and Tulsa.
He is represented in hundreds of private and
public collections worldwide.

Cover Artist: Otto Duecker
Photographer: Rick Stiller
Illustrator: Jim Richey
Food Stylists: Stephanie Coon, Sadie Fuller
Props: Kathleen Brannen
      Patricia Breckinridge
      First Data Corp
      Mary "Tucky" Hazen
      Steve and Barbara Martin
      Melba Richey
      Mark Thomas
      John Walton
Wine Consultant: Milton Leiter

MISSION STATEMENT

The Junior League of Tulsa, Inc., is an organization of women committed to promoting voluntarism, developing the potential of women and improving communities through the effective action and leadership of trained volunteers. Its purpose is exclusively educational and charitable. The Junior League of Tulsa, Inc., reaches out to women of all races, religions, and national origins who demonstrate an interest in and commitment to voluntarism.

2000–2001 COOKBOOK COMMITTEE

Production Committee
CHAIR:
Stephanie Coon
VICE-CHAIR:
Sadie Fuller
COMMITTEE:
Elisa Bowen
Liz Carson
Amy Koontz
Denise Piland
Meganne Pracht
Bette Richter
Bryn Stratton
Anne Westfield
BOARD ADVISOR:
Deidra Kirtley

Marketing Committee
CHAIR:
Kim Smith
VICE-CHAIR:
Anne Darnell
COMMITTEE:
Lynne Beeson
Mandy Brueck
Jayme Burton
Regan Farris
Tiffany Glass
Jennifer Leahy
Lisa Lilly
Jacalyn Peter
Denise Rigdon
BOARD ADVISOR:
Sarah Jane McKinney Blevins
SUSTAINING ADVISORS:
Caroline Crain
Susan McCalman

Oil & Vinegar highlights favorite recipes from the League's earlier cookbooks.

Denotes recipes from
The Junior League of Tulsa Cookbook, Circa 1949

Denotes recipes from *Cook's Collage,* 1978

The Junior League of Tulsa

Since our beginning in 1923, the Junior League of Tulsa has established nearly sixty different community projects. We have researched, initiated, raised money for, piloted, and/or staffed each new project. We have also collaborated with many agencies to make existing community programs even better. Once a project has become self supporting, we then turn it over to the community.

Arts Council of Tulsa, Inc.
AVID Readers
Books to Shut-ins
Breast Cancer Awareness
Cardiopulmonary Resuscitation (CPR)
Career Education for Life's Sake
Case Aid
Centennial Time Capsule Project
Child Abuse Network
Child Lures
Children's Medical Center
Children's Museum, Philbrook
Laura Dester Children's Shelter
Christmas in April Tulsa
Citizens Information Service
Club Foot Clinic, St. John Medical
    Center
Community Arts Survey
Community Resource Center
    for the Arts & Humanities
Court School
Diagnostic Nursery,
    Children's Medical Center
Domestic Violence Intervention
    Services
Dress For Success
Eating Disorders Awareness
Excellence in Education
First Start with
    Community Action Project
Focus on Art
Frances E. Willard Home
Gemini (Tulsa Public Schools Arts
    Enrichment)
Gilcrease American Heritage
    Society
Gilcrease Arch Aides
Gilcrease Docent Program
Going to Bat for Tulsa's Kids
    Mentoring Program

Hard of Hearing School,
    University of Tulsa
Harmon Science Center
Historic Preservation/Art Deco
Historic Preservation/Oral Histories
Juvenile Bureau
Juvenile Justice Center
Leadership Tulsa, Inc.
Literacy Project
Mayfest
Model Day Care Curriculum
Natural History Exhibit, Tulsa Zoo
Oxley Nature Center
Parenting Coalition Activity
Pediatric Enrichment Program
Philbrook Docent Program
Philbrook Junior Gallery
Philbrook Junior Research
    & Exhibit Gallery
Philharmonic Youth Concerts
Preschool Deaf Therapy,
    Children's Medical Center
Preschool Screening and TRY
Program Reach Out (PRO)
Puppetry Program, Radio Broadcasts
    for Children
Red Cross Bundles for America
Ronald McDonald House
Science Enrichment Project,
    Tulsa Public Schools
Tulsa History from A to Z
Tulsa Summer Arts
Victim Witness
Vision Screening
Volunteer Bureau
Volunteers in the Library
Woman to Woman
Women's Resource Center
Youth Services of Tulsa

Foreword

The Junior League of Tulsa is proud to present **Oil & Vinegar**,
an emulsion of recipes from its members, friends, and families.
In the early 1920s, Tulsa was known as the "Oil Capital of the World."
People flocked to Tulsa by the thousands, lured by the hope of striking
it rich with oil. These ambitious families brought various traditions, legacies,
and dreams, creating a culinary melting pot.

The recipes in **Oil & Vinegar** were selected from more than 2,000 submissions.
They are designed to inspire you to make your everyday cooking a special occasion.
We now live life at such a hectic pace that gathering with family and
friends should always be a special occasion.

By purchasing, giving, and using **Oil & Vinegar**, you not only are expanding
the possibilities in your kitchen; you are also expanding the possibilities
for the Tulsa community. Since 1923, the Junior League of Tulsa, Inc.,
has been an organization of women committed to promoting voluntarism,
developing the potential of women, and improving the community
through effective action and leadership of trained volunteers.
Its purpose is exclusively educational and charitable.

Tulsa may no longer be the "Oil Capital of the World," but we are sure
you will strike it rich in your kitchen with the selections within these pages.

CONTENTS

APPETIZERS
BEVERAGES

Asian Fusion Pork Appetizer

2 pounds pork tenderloin, trimmed
$^1/4$ cup soy sauce
$^1/4$ cup packed brown sugar
2 tablespoons sherry
1 teaspoon onion powder
1 teaspoon cinnamon
2 tablespoons olive oil

Place the pork in a shallow nonreactive dish. Combine the soy sauce, brown sugar, sherry, onion powder, cinnamon and olive oil in a small bowl and mix well. Pour over the pork and marinate, covered, in the refrigerator for 2 hours or longer. Drain the pork, reserving the marinade.

Grill the pork over low heat with the grill lid closed for 30 to 35 minutes or until cooked through, turning and basting frequently with the reserved marinade. Discard any remaining marinade. Remove from the heat and let stand, covered with foil, for 10 to 15 minutes. Cut into thin diagonal slices and serve hot or cold with Ginger Scallion Sauce (below), Champagne Mustard Sauce (page 113), Plum Lemon Sauce (page 114), or Thai Dipping Sauce (page 117).

Serves 12   *Photograph for this recipe appears on page 10.*

Ginger Scallion Sauce

$^1/4$ cup soy sauce
2 tablespoons rice wine vinegar
4 scallions, minced
4 teaspoons minced fresh gingerroot
cayenne pepper to taste

Combine the soy sauce, vinegar, scallions, gingerroot and cayenne pepper in a small bowl and mix well. Store, covered, in the refrigerator.

Makes $^3/4$ cup   *Photograph for this recipe appears on page 10.*

BACON-WRAPPED PORTOBELLOS AND PLUMS

1 cup red or white wine
24 dried plums, apricots or apple slices
1 large or 2 small portobello mushrooms (about 8 ounces)
12 bacon slices, cut into halves

Bring the wine to a boil in a small saucepan over high heat. Add the plums and remove from the heat. Let stand for 30 minutes.

Cut the mushrooms into quarters. Cut each quarter into $1/4$-inch slices for a total of 24 pieces. Drain the plums and discard the wine or reserve it for another use.

Arrange 1 plum and 1 slice of mushroom on a half-slice of bacon. Wrap the bacon around the plum and mushroom slice and secure with a wooden pick. Repeat with the remaining ingredients.

Arrange the bacon rolls in a broiler pan. Broil 8 inches from the heat source for 2 to 3 minutes on each side or until the bacon is cooked through. Serve hot or cold.

Serves 6

PROSCIUTTO PURSES

6 (3×6-inch) thin prosciutto slices
$1/4$ cup ricotta cheese
1 tablespoon minced fresh basil
minced chives (optional)
salt to taste

Cut the prosciutto slices into halves. Combine the cheese, basil, chives and salt in a small bowl and mix well.

Spoon 1 teaspoon of the cheese mixture into the center of each prosciutto slice. Roll each slice to enclose the filling and twist the ends in a candy wrapper fashion. Arrange on a platter to serve.

Serves 6   *Photograph for this recipe appears on page 10.*

HELPFUL HINT

Prosciutto is ham that has been aged and air-dried after being cured in a spicy brine. It should be firm but chewy and rose-colored with a slight gloss. The flavor should be both peppery and salty with a subtle nutty element.

STUFFED PORTOBELLO MUSHROOM CAPS

HELPFUL HINT

Portobello mushrooms can be stuffed, grilled or roasted with extra-virgin olive oil. They are milder in flavor than porcini mushrooms, yet still have depth of flavor. There are both wild and common cultivated varieties.

4 portobello mushrooms with stems
1 teaspoon minced garlic
1 teaspoon minced shallot
2 tablespoons butter, melted
1/2 cup white wine
1 cup heavy cream
1 cup grated Parmesan cheese
1 pound spinach, rinsed, stemmed
salt and white pepper to taste
1/2 cup Danish bleu cheese, crumbled
1/2 cup toasted bread crumbs

Remove and finely chop the mushroom stems. Sauté the stems, garlic and shallot in the butter in a large nonstick skillet over medium heat just until tender.

Add the wine and cook over medium heat, stirring to loosen any browned bits from the bottom of the skillet. Stir in the cream and simmer until the mixture is reduced and thickened, stirring occasionally. Stir in the Parmesan cheese.

Add the spinach and cook until the spinach wilts and the mixture forms a thick paste, stirring frequently. Season with salt and pepper.

Spoon the spinach mixture into the mushroom caps and arrange in a baking dish. Bake at 350 degrees for 20 minutes or until the mushroom caps are tender. Sprinkle with the Danish bleu cheese and bread crumbs. Bake for 2 to 3 minutes longer or until the cheese melts.

Serves 4

RED POTATOES WITH WALNUTS AND GORGONZOLA CHEESE

20 red new potatoes, cut into halves
salt and pepper to taste
1 teaspoon thyme
2 tablespoons olive oil
4 ounces cream cheese, softened
1 1/2 ounces Gorgonzola cheese
4 slices bacon, crisp-fried, crumbled
1/4 cup sour cream
1/4 cup coarsely chopped walnuts
Worcestershire sauce and Tabasco sauce to taste
1 1/2 tablespoons minced chives

Scoop out the center of each potato half, reserving the centers for another use. Toss the potato halves with salt, pepper, thyme and olive oil in a medium bowl. Arrange the potatoes cut side down on a nonstick baking sheet. Bake at 300 degrees for 15 minutes or until the potatoes are tender and golden brown.

Beat the cream cheese in a medium mixing bowl until smooth. Add the Gorgonzola cheese, bacon, sour cream and walnuts and mix well. Season with Worcestershire sauce and Tabasco sauce.

Spoon the cheese mixture into each hot potato half , or pipe, using a pastry bag fitted with a large tip. Sprinkle with the chives.

Makes 40 hors d'oeuvre

HELPFUL HINT

One of Italy's oldest cheeses, Gorgonzola is rich and pungent with blue or green veins and a golden curd. Try it as a dessert with ripe juicy pears and a glass of hearty red wine.

In 1915, the Cushing Oil Field near Tulsa attained a peak gross production of 305,000 barrels of crude oil per day.

SPINACH STRUDEL

$1/2$ onion, chopped
1 tablespoon butter
4 strudel pastry sheets
$1/2$ cup (1 stick) butter or margarine, melted
$1/2$ cup bread crumbs
1 (10-ounce) package frozen chopped spinach, cooked, drained
3 ounces cream cheese, softened
1 tablespoon seasoned salt

Sauté the onion in 1 tablespoon butter in a small skillet over medium heat until tender.

Unfold 1 pastry sheet onto a damp kitchen towel. Brush the surface with $1/3$ of the melted butter and sprinkle evenly with $1/3$ of the bread crumbs. Layer a pastry sheet over the top, brushing with half the remaining melted butter and sprinkling with half the remaining bread crumbs. Repeat the process with a pastry sheet and the remaining melted butter and bread crumbs. Layer the remaining pastry sheet over the top.

Combine the spinach, onion mixture and cream cheese in a small bowl and mix well. Spoon the mixture along a lengthwise edge of the top strudel sheet. Sprinkle evenly with the seasoned salt. Fold in the short ends of the pastry 1 inch toward the center to keep the filling intact. Roll as for a jelly roll to enclose the filling using the kitchen towel as an aid.

Place seam side down in a buttered baking pan. Bake at 400 degrees for 20 to 30 minutes or until golden brown. Cool slightly on a wire rack. Slice into $3/4$-inch slices to serve.

Serves 12

POTSTICKERS

POTSTICKERS
12 ounces ground pork or chicken
3 scallions, cut into 1-inch pieces
1 carrot, cut into 1-inch pieces
1 (8-ounce) can water chestnuts, drained
1 egg
white pepper to taste
hot chili oil and soy sauce to taste
1 package of won ton wrappers, cut into circles
vegetable oil for frying

SPICY SAUCE
1 tablespoon minced garlic
4 1/2 teaspoons sesame oil
2 teaspoons (or more) hot chili oil
1/2 teaspoon white pepper
1/3 cup sugar
1/4 cup rice vinegar
2 tablespoons dark soy sauce
2 tablespoons light soy sauce
toasted sesame seeds to taste
chopped gingerroot to taste

HELPFUL HINT

When cooking potstickers, swirl them gently from side to side to coat the bottoms of the won ton wrappers with oil and prevent them from sticking to the pan.

FOR THE POTSTICKERS, combine the ground pork, scallions, carrot, water chestnuts, egg, white pepper, chili oil and soy sauce in a food processor and process until well mixed. Spoon 1 heaping teaspoon of the mixture into the center of each won ton circle. Moisten the edges of each wrapper with water and fold over to enclose the filling; press to seal. Cover completed potstickers with a damp towel.

Heat a small amount of vegetable oil in a large skillet over medium-high heat until hot. Place the potstickers pouch side down in the hot oil and cook until golden brown. Add a small amount of water and steam, covered, for 10 minutes or until cooked through. Remove the potstickers and drain on paper towels.

FOR THE SAUCE, combine the garlic, sesame oil, chili oil, white pepper, sugar, rice vinegar, soy sauces, sesame seeds and gingerroot in a small bowl and mix well. Serve with the potstickers.

Serves 6

BRUSCHETTA

HELPFUL HINT

In Italy, bruschetta is traditionally a workman's midday snack. Bruschetta can be topped with an endless array of ingredient combinations, such as black olive tapenade, diced roasted bell peppers with crumbled goat cheese, or drained canned tuna and capers. Try mashed white beans and prosciutto, strips of Parmigiano-Reggiano cheese, or a garlic clove rubbed over the toast and followed by a generous drizzle of olive oil.

6 to 8 Roma tomatoes, chopped
2 tablespoons minced garlic
2 tablespoons minced onion or shallot
3/4 cup fresh basil, chopped
1 teaspoon fresh lemon juice
1/2 cup olive oil
salt and pepper to taste
1 loaf French bread, sliced, toasted

Combine the tomatoes, garlic, onion, basil, lemon juice and olive oil in a medium bowl and mix well. Season with salt and pepper. Spread on the toast slices and serve at room temperature.

Serves 6 to 8

APRICOT BOATS WITH CHIVE GOAT CHEESE

30 dried apricots or plums
1 cup white wine
2 tablespoons minced fresh chives
6 ounces goat cheese
3 to 4 whole chives

Simmer the apricots in the wine in a small saucepan over medium heat for 10 minutes. Remove from the heat and let stand, covered, for 10 to 15 minutes. Drain the apricots, reserving 2 tablespoons of the wine.

Combine the minced chives, reserved wine and the goat cheese in a small bowl and mix well. Spoon a heaping 1/2 teaspoon of the cheese mixture on top of each apricot. Cut the whole chives into 1/2-inch pieces. Top each apricot with 1 chive piece.

Serves 10 to 15

MUSHROOM CROUSTADES

1/4 cup (1/2 stick) butter, melted
24 slices bread, crusts trimmed
1/4 cup (1/2 stick) butter
3 tablespoons finely chopped onion
8 ounces mushrooms, finely chopped
2 tablespoons flour
1 cup whipping cream
1/2 teaspoon salt
1/8 teaspoon cayenne pepper
1 tablespoon finely chopped parsley
1 1/2 tablespoons chopped chives
1/2 teaspoon lemon juice
butter
grated Parmesan cheese

Brush 24 miniature muffin cups with the melted butter. Cut the bread slices into rounds with a fluted 3-inch cutter. Press the rounds gently into the muffin cups. Bake at 400 degrees for 10 minutes or until golden brown. Remove from the pans and cool on a wire rack.

Melt 1/4 cup butter in a heavy skillet over medium heat and heat until foamy. Add the onion and cook for 4 minutes, stirring constantly. Add the mushrooms and toss to coat well. Cook for 15 minutes or until the moisture is evaporated, stirring occasionally.

Remove from the heat and stir in the flour. Add the cream and bring the mixture to a boil over medium-high heat, stirring constantly. Simmer for 1 to 3 minutes, stirring frequently. Remove from the heat and stir in the salt, cayenne pepper, parsley, chives and lemon juice.

Spoon the mushroom mixture into the toast cups. Dot with additional butter and sprinkle with Parmesan cheese. Arrange on a nonstick baking sheet. Bake at 350 degrees for 10 minutes. Broil just until brown.

You may make the filling in advance and store in the refrigerator until needed.

Serves 12

Coconut Shrimp

Seasoning Mixture

1 tablespoon cayenne pepper
2 1/4 teaspoons salt
1 1/2 teaspoons paprika
1 1/2 teaspoons black pepper

1 1/4 teaspoons garlic powder
3/4 teaspoon onion powder
3/4 teaspoon thyme
3/4 teaspoon oregano

Shrimp

1 1/4 cups flour
3 egg yolks
3/4 cup beer
2 egg whites
1/2 cup flour

24 large peeled shrimp
  (about 12 ounces)
5 cups flaked coconut
peanut oil

Marmalade Sauce

3/4 cup orange marmalade
2 1/2 tablespoons Dijon mustard

2 1/2 tablespoons prepared
  horseradish, drained

FOR THE SEASONING MIXTURE, mix the cayenne pepper, salt, paprika, black pepper, garlic powder, onion powder, thyme and oregano in a small bowl.

FOR THE SHRIMP, combine 2 teaspoons of the seasoning mixture with 1 1/4 cups flour, egg yolks and beer in a medium bowl and whisk until smooth. Beat the egg whites in a small bowl until stiff peaks form. Fold into the beer mixture gently. Chill, covered, for 30 minutes.

Combine 1/2 cup flour and 1 1/2 teaspoons of the seasoning mixture together. Toss the shrimp in the remaining seasoning mixture and then in the seasoned flour mixture to coat. Dip the shrimp into the beer mixture and roll in the coconut. Deep-fry in hot peanut oil until golden brown. Drain on paper towels.

FOR THE SAUCE, combine the marmalade, Dijon mustard and horseradish in a small bowl and mix well. Serve as a dip with the fried shrimp.

Do not use dark beer in this recipe.

Serves 8

SOPHISTICATED SHRIMP

VINEGAR MARINADE
1 1/2 cups vegetable oil
3/4 cup white vinegar
7 or 8 bay leaves
2 1/2 teaspoons celery seeds
1 (3-ounce) jar capers
Tabasco sauce to taste

SHRIMP
shrimp and crab boil to taste
1/2 lemon, sliced
2 1/2 pounds unpeeled medium or large shrimp
2 cups thinly sliced yellow onion

FOR THE MARINADE, combine the vegetable oil, vinegar, bay leaves, celery seeds, undrained capers and Tabasco sauce in a shallow glass dish.

FOR THE SHRIMP, combine the shrimp and crab boil and lemon slices with enough water to cover the shrimp in a medium saucepan and bring to a boil. Add the shrimp and cook just until the shrimp are opaque. Drain and cool slightly. Peel the shrimp.

Add the cooked shrimp and onion to the marinade and marinate, covered, in the refrigerator for 24 hours to 1 week.

Serves 10 to 12

HELPFUL HINT

If you can't find the commercial version, try preparing your own Shrimp and Crab Boil. Combine 1 tablespoon celery seeds, 1 tablespoon whole black peppercorns, 6 bay leaves, 1/2 teaspoon whole cardamom, 1/2 teaspoon mustard seeds, 4 whole cloves, 1 teaspoon sweet Hungarian paprika and a dash of salt in a small bowl and mix well.

CHEESE WAFERS

1 pound Cheddar cheese, shredded
1 cup (2 sticks) butter, softened
2 cups flour
1 teaspoon salt
1/4 cup minced onion

Let the cheese stand at room temperature for several hours to soften. Combine the cheese and butter in a large bowl and beat until smooth. Add the flour gradually, mixing well after each addition to form a stiff dough. Add the salt and onion and mix well.

Shape the dough into a log 1 1/2 inches in diameter. Wrap in waxed paper and refrigerate for 8 hours or longer. Cut into 1/4-inch slices and arrange 2 inches apart on a nonstick baking sheet. Bake at 350 degrees for 8 minutes. Serve hot or at room temperature.

You may prepare the wafers in advance and freeze them. Thaw slightly and bake as directed.

Makes 4 dozen

PECANS PIQUANT

3 tablespoons butter, melted
3 tablespoons Worcestershire sauce
3 dashes of Tabasco sauce
8 ounces pecan halves
salt to taste

Combine the butter, Worcestershire sauce and Tabasco sauce in a medium bowl and mix well. Add the pecans and toss to coat evenly. Spread the pecans on a baking sheet lined with baking parchment and sprinkle with salt. Roast at 300 degrees for 10 to 12 minutes. Cool completely. Store in an airtight container.

Makes about 2 cups

ARTICHOKE DIP

1 (14-ounce) can artichoke hearts, drained
1 cup mayonnaise
1 cup grated Parmesan cheese
1/2 cup (or more) shredded Parmesan cheese
8 ounces cream cheese, softened
1/2 cup sour cream
2 garlic cloves, crushed
2 teaspoons garlic powder
1/2 teaspoon dillweed
1/2 teaspoon Worcestershire sauce
2 teaspoons freshly grated Parmesan cheese

Chop the artichoke hearts finely. Combine the artichokes, mayonnaise, Parmesan cheeses, cream cheese and sour cream in a medium bowl and mix well.

Add the garlic, garlic powder, dillweed and Worcestershire sauce and mix well. Spoon the mixture into a baking dish and sprinkle evenly with 2 teaspoons Parmesan cheese.

Bake at 350 degrees for 20 to 30 minutes or until hot and bubbly. Serve with toasted pita bread triangles or crackers or in a hollowed sourdough bread bowl.

You may double the recipe for larger gatherings.

Serves 12

In 1909, the Tulsa City Directory listed 126 oil companies with offices in Tulsa. By 1930, over 800 oil companies were headquartered in Tulsa.

BETTER-THAN-EVER BLEU CHEESE DIP

HELPFUL HINT

Bleu cheese refers to blue-veined cheeses of many varieties.

Gorgonzola cheese, a specialty of Lombardy, is named for a town just outside of Milan, Italy. It is a mild, creamy, pale yellow blue-veined cheese made from fresh cow's milk.

Maytag cheese is an American blue-veined cheese, with a fairly firm consistency. It is generally milder than its European counterparts.

Roquefort cheese, a French cheese made from sheep's milk, has a creamy consistency and a rich, sharp taste.

Stilton cheese is an English blue-veined cheese made from cow's milk. It is firm and slightly crumbly.

8 ounces cream cheese with chives, softened
8 ounces bleu cheese
juice of 1 lemon
$1/8$ teaspoon ground red pepper
1 to 2 teaspoons Worcestershire sauce
$1/4$ teaspoon tarragon

Combine the cream cheese, bleu cheese, lemon juice, red pepper, Worcestershire sauce and tarragon in a medium bowl and mix well. Serve with melba rounds, chips or celery. For a bleu cheese salad dressing, add enough cream to the finished dip to make of the desired consistency.

Serves 12

GREAT SPINACH DIP

1 (10-ounce) package frozen chopped spinach, thawed
8 ounces cream cheese, softened
1 (10-ounce) can diced tomatoes with green chiles
3 cups shredded Colby Jack cheese
1 tablespoon lemon pepper
$1/2$ cup minced onion

Drain the spinach, pressing out the excess moisture. Combine the spinach and cream cheese in a large bowl and mix well. Add the tomatoes with green chiles, Colby Jack cheese, lemon pepper and onion and mix well.

Spoon into a greased 9×9-inch baking dish. Bake at 350 degrees for 20 minutes or until bubbly. Serve warm with pita chips or corn chips.

Serves 10 to 15

CURRIED SPINACH AND APPLE DIP

2 (10-ounce) packages frozen chopped spinach, thawed
1 cup mayonnaise
curry powder to taste
1 large unpeeled apple, cored, finely chopped
1 cup Major Grey's chutney
1 cup chopped peanuts

Drain the spinach, pressing out the excess moisture. Combine with the mayonnaise and curry powder in a medium bowl and mix well. Add the apple, chutney and peanuts and mix well. Chill, covered, for 8 hours or longer. Serve with crackers, crudités or pita toasts.

Serves 16

Shrimp Dip

2 pounds frozen cooked shrimp, thawed
8 ounces cream cheese, softened
1/2 cup mayonnaise
1 cup Thousand Island salad dressing
1/4 cup minced green onions
1/2 small onion, grated
4 teaspoons Tabasco sauce
1 tablespoon seasoned salt
1 tablespoon prepared horseradish

Pulse the shrimp in a food processor until coarsely chopped. Combine the cream cheese, mayonnaise and salad dressing in a medium bowl and mix well. Stir in the shrimp, green onions, onion, Tabasco sauce, seasoned salt and horseradish. Adjust the seasonings to taste. Chill, covered, for 8 hours or longer to blend the flavors. Serve with crackers or toasts.

Serves 8 to 10

Guacamole

3 large ripe avocados, cut into quarters
1 medium tomato, seeded, finely chopped
1/3 medium white onion, finely chopped
1 fresh large jalapeño chile, seeded, minced
5 large garlic cloves, minced
1/2 teaspoon (or more) kosher salt
1/2 teaspoon cracked black pepper
1/2 cup fresh cilantro, chopped
juice of 1 to 2 limes

Combine the avocados, tomato, onion, jalapeño chile, garlic, salt, pepper, cilantro and lime juice in a glass or ceramic serving bowl. Mash with a potato masher or large fork just until mixed, leaving the mixture somewhat chunky for the best flavor and texture.

This is a great topping for Tortilla Soup with Cilantro and Green Chiles (page 103).

Makes 3 cups

BLACK BEAN SALSA

2 (15-ounce) cans black beans, rinsed, drained
1 (16-ounce) can whole kernel corn, rinsed, drained
2 large tomatoes, seeded, chopped
1 large avocado, chopped
1 purple onion, chopped
1/8 to 1/4 cup chopped fresh cilantro
3 to 4 tablespoons lime juice
2 tablespoons olive oil
1 tablespoon red wine vinegar
1 teaspoon salt
1/2 teaspoon pepper

Combine the black beans, corn, tomatoes, avocado, onion and cilantro in a medium serving bowl and toss to mix. Combine the lime juice, olive oil, vinegar, salt and pepper in a small bowl and whisk until well blended. Pour over the black bean mixture and mix well. Chill, covered, until serving time.

Makes 6 cups

HELPFUL HINT

Serve Black Bean Salsa with tortilla chips as a dip or as a topping for chicken, beef, pork, or fish. The mixture also makes a good vegetarian filling for burritos with shredded Monterey Jack cheese.

Confetti Pineapple and Onion Salsa

1 large pineapple, finely chopped
1 onion, finely chopped
6 tablespoons minced fresh mint
2 tablespoons minced serrano or jalapeño chile
salt and pepper to taste

Combine the pineapple, onion, mint and serrano chile in a nonreactive bowl and mix well. Season with salt and pepper to taste. Chill, covered, for 6 to 8 hours. Serve with tortilla chips.

Serves 6 to 8

Salsa Fresca

8 mixed jalapeño and other chile peppers, seeded
1 cup chopped red onion
1 cup fresh cilantro leaves, stemmed
3 garlic cloves, cut into quarters
juice of 1 lemon
juice of 1/2 lime
1 1/2 tablespoons vegetable oil
2 teaspoons salt
6 Roma tomatoes, cut into quarters

Combine the chile peppers, onion, cilantro, garlic, lemon juice, lime juice, vegetable oil and salt in a food processor. Pulse 4 to 6 times or until the ingredients are chopped and mixed but still chunky. Add the tomatoes and pulse once or twice or just until combined. Serve with chips.

Makes 8 cups

PEPPERS PROVENÇAL

1/4 cup olive oil
2 tablespoons butter
2 cups thinly sliced white or Vidalia onions
2 red bell peppers, julienned
1/2 teaspoon herbes de Provence
salt and pepper to taste
4 garlic cloves, minced
1/2 cup thinly sliced fresh basil

Heat the olive oil and butter in a heavy skillet over medium heat until the butter is melted. Add the onions and bell peppers and sprinkle with the herbes de Provence and salt and pepper to taste; stir to mix well. Simmer for 45 minutes or until the vegetables are tender, stirring frequently. Add the garlic and basil and cook for 5 minutes longer. Remove from the heat and let stand until cool.

Drain the excess oil and serve with crackers or crusty bread slices.

Makes 2 cups

HELPFUL HINT

Herbes de Provence is a typical dried herb blend of the Provence region of south central France. This blend may include rosemary, thyme, savory, oregano, basil, sage, marjoram, fennel, mint, and/or lavender blossoms. Crushing the dried herbs with a mortar and pestle, or in the palm of the hand, is the best way to release their flavor.

BLACK OLIVE TAPENADE

1 (16-ounce) can pitted black olives, drained
1/8 purple onion, finely chopped
4 ounces fresh mushroom caps, finely chopped
1 ounce tiny capers
1/4 cup freshly grated Parmesan cheese
1 tablespoon Dijon mustard
1/4 cup (or more) Italian salad dressing
Juice of 1/2 large lemon (or more), strained

Chop the olives finely. Combine the olives, onion, mushrooms, capers, cheese, Dijon mustard, salad dressing and lemon juice in a medium bowl and mix well. Add additional salad dressing and lemon juice if needed for the desired consistency. Adjust the seasonings. Chill, covered, for 3 hours or longer. Serve with garlic or onion bagel chips or spread on cold smoked salmon and roll to enclose the tapenade.

Serves 20 to 30

CHUTNEY BALL

HELPFUL HINT

Chutney is good served with hot or cold roasted meats or poultry. For a different twist, serve it on a hamburger, in an omelet, or with cheese on a cracker.

16 ounces cream cheese, softened
1 tablespoon curry powder
1/2 cup sour cream
1/2 cup chopped dry-roasted peanuts
1/2 cup chopped raisins
1/4 cup chopped green onions
1 (9-ounce) jar Major Grey's chutney
1 parsley sprig

Beat the cream cheese in a medium bowl until light and fluffy. Add the curry powder and sour cream and mix well. Stir in the peanuts, raisins and green onions. Shape into a ball and place on a serving plate. Chill, covered, until serving time. Top with the chutney and parsley sprig just before serving. Serve with wheat crackers.

Makes 4 to 5 cups

FESTIVE FETA CHEESE BALL

1 garlic clove, minced
3 medium scallions, chopped
16 ounces cream cheese, softened
8 ounces feta cheese, crumbled
3 tablespoons sour cream
1 1/2 teaspoons dillweed
1 1/2 teaspoons pepper
1 teaspoon oregano
salt to taste
1/4 cup finely chopped radish
1/4 cup finely chopped fresh parsley

Combine the garlic, scallions, cream cheese, feta cheese and sour cream in a medium bowl and mix well. Add the dillweed, pepper, oregano and salt and mix well. Toss the radish and parsley in a shallow dish. Shape the cheese mixture into a ball and roll in the radish mixture, coating evenly. Chill, covered, on a decorative plate until serving time. Serve with crackers.

Serves 8

CHICKEN PÂTÉ

1 1/2 cups chopped cooked chicken breast
3 tablespoons chopped onion
2 tablespoons mayonnaise
1/2 teaspoon hot pepper sauce
8 ounces Neufchâtel cheese, softened
2 tablespoons dry sherry
2 teaspoons lemon juice
1/8 teaspoon nutmeg
1/4 teaspoon paprika

Combine the chicken, onion, mayonnaise, pepper sauce, cheese, sherry, lemon juice and nutmeg in a food processor. Process until smooth, stopping once or twice to scrape down the side of the bowl with a spatula.

Line a mold with plastic wrap or spray with cooking spray. Spoon the mixture into the prepared mold. Chill, covered, for 8 hours or longer. Unmold onto a serving platter and sprinkle with the paprika. Serve with crackers.

Serves 8 to 12

GOAT CHEESE SPREAD WITH WALNUTS AND SUN-DRIED TOMATOES

4 ounces Montrachet or other goat cheese, softened
2/3 cup walnuts, coarsely chopped, toasted
4 oil-pack sun-dried tomatoes, drained, coarsely chopped
1 large garlic clove, coarsely chopped
1 teaspoon extra-virgin olive oil
1/4 teaspoon thyme
salt and coarsely ground pepper to taste

Combine the goat cheese, walnuts, tomatoes, garlic, olive oil, thyme, salt and pepper in a food processor. Pulse until well mixed but still slightly chunky in texture. Spoon into a serving bowl or a mold lined with plastic wrap. Chill for 10 minutes or until firm.

Unmold onto a serving plate. Serve with Pita Crisps (below) and/or fruit, such as red or white seedless grapes, tart apples or Bosc pear slices.

Makes 1 1/2 cups

PITA CRISPS

6 (6-inch) white or whole wheat pita bread rounds
1/4 cup (1/2 stick) butter, melted
3 tablespoons olive oil
1/4 cup sesame seeds
1 tablespoon thyme
1 1/2 tablespoons freshly ground pepper
1/2 cup freshly grated Parmesan cheese

Trim the edge of each pita bread round and cut the rounds into quarters. Separate the tops from the bottoms. Combine the butter and olive oil in a small bowl and whisk until smooth. Brush over both sides of the pita quarters. Arrange the pieces on 2 nonstick baking sheets.

Combine the sesame seeds, thyme and pepper in a small bowl and mix well. Sprinkle the mixture evenly over the tops of the bread pieces. Sprinkle evenly with the cheese.

Position 1 baking sheet on the top rack of the oven and 1 baking sheet on the bottom rack of the oven. Bake at 350 degrees for 8 minutes. Switch the positions of the baking sheets and bake for 6 minutes longer or until toasted and crisp.

Makes 4 dozen

SUN-DRIED TOMATO CHEESE TORTE

1/2 cup oil-pack sun-dried tomatoes, drained, chopped
1 cup freshly grated Parmesan cheese
8 ounces cream cheese, softened
4 ounces goat cheese, crumbled
1/4 cup (1/2 stick) butter or margarine, softened
1/2 cup freshly grated Parmesan cheese
2 to 3 garlic cloves, minced
1/4 cup minced fresh parsley
1 tablespoon minced fresh basil
1/2 teaspoon freshly ground pepper

Line a 3-cup mold or 4-cup glass measuring cup with plastic wrap or cheesecloth, allowing 5 to 6 inches to hang over the edge. Spray the plastic wrap with nonstick cooking spray. Sprinkle the sun-dried tomatoes into the mold.

Combine 1 cup Parmesan cheese, cream cheese, goat cheese and butter in a mixing bowl and beat until smooth. Reserve 1 cup of the mixture. Spoon the remaining mixture over the tomatoes in the mold.

Mix the reserved cheese mixture with 1/2 cup Parmesan cheese, garlic, parsley, basil and pepper in a mixing bowl until well blended. Spread evenly over the cheese mixture in the mold.

Fold the excess plastic wrap over the top. Chill for up to 8 hours. Unmold onto a serving platter and serve with crackers.

Serves 20

BEACH BALL

1/2 cup heavy cream
1/3 cup crème de cacao
1/4 cup strawberry daiquiri mix
2 tablespoons Kahlúa
ice cubes

Combine the heavy cream, crème de cacao, daiquiri mix and Kahlúa in a blender. Fill with ice cubes and blend until smooth.

Serves 4 to 6

BUSHWHACKERS

3 tablespoons Bailey's Irish cream
2 tablespoons Kahlúa
2 tablespoons amaretto
2 tablespoons vodka
1 tablespoon crème de cacao
ice
whipped cream
nutmeg to taste

Combine the Irish cream, Kahlúa, amaretto, vodka and crème de cacao in a blender. Fill with ice and blend until smooth. Pour into glasses and top with whipped cream and nutmeg.

Serves 2 to 4

Chocolate Martini

1 jigger vanilla vodka
1 jigger white chocolate liqueur

1 jigger Godiva chocolate liqueur
1 splash crème de cacao

Combine equal measures of the vodka and liqueurs in a shaker. Add the crème de cacao and shake until well combined. Serve in chilled glasses.

Serves 1

Custom Irish Cream

1 3/4 cups Irish whiskey
1 (14-ounce) can sweetened
   condensed milk
1 cup heavy cream
1 cup egg substitute

2 tablespoons chocolate syrup
2 teaspoons instant coffee crystals
1 teaspoon vanilla extract
1/4 teaspoon almond extract

Combine the whiskey, condensed milk, heavy cream, egg substitute, chocolate syrup, coffee crystals, vanilla and almond extract in a blender; process until smooth.

Store, tightly covered, in the refrigerator for up to 3 weeks. Stir before serving.

Serves 4

The Reviver

3/4 cup fresh orange juice
3/4 cup cranberry juice cocktail
1/4 cup fresh grapefruit juice
1/4 cup gold tequila

4 teaspoons fresh lime juice
shaved ice
lime slices

Combine the orange juice, cranberry juice cocktail, grapefruit juice, tequila and lime juice in a small pitcher and stir until well blended. Fill 2 wine glasses with shaved ice and pour the juice mixture over the ice. Garnish with lime slices.

Serves 2

VODKA INFUSION FOR BLOODY MARY

HELPFUL HINT

To peel pearl onions, trim the ends of each onion with a small, sharp knife. Bring enough water to cover the onions to a boil in a medium saucepan over high heat. Add the onions and boil for 2 minutes; drain. When the onions are cool enough to handle, slide off the skins by pressing the onions gently with the fingers.

VODKA INFUSION
10 ounces pearl onions, peeled
1 celery heart with leaves, cut into 1-inch pieces
1 (16-ounce) jar sweet cherry peppers
1 liter vodka

BLOODY MARY
1 (2-ounce) jigger vodka infusion
1/2 cup Bloody Mary mix or Tomato Juice Cocktail (page 37)
2 teaspoons lime juice
1 teaspoon Worcestershire sauce
salt and pepper to taste
hot pepper sauce to taste
ice
1 celery rib

FOR THE INFUSION, layer the onions, celery pieces and cherry peppers in a large sun tea jar. Pour the vodka over the top. Cover and let stand for 24 to 48 hours to allow flavors to infuse.

FOR THE BLOODY MARY, combine the vodka infusion, Bloody Mary mix, lime juice, Worcestershire sauce, salt and pepper to taste, pepper sauce and ice in a shaker and shake to blend. Strain into a chilled glass and serve with a celery rib.

Serves 1

TOMATO JUICE COCKTAIL

1 1/4 teaspoons celery salt
1 1/2 teaspoons prepared horseradish
2 tablespoons lemon juice
1/2 cup orange juice
1/3 cup Worcestershire sauce
1 1/2 teaspoons salt
1 1/4 tablespoons sugar
8 cups tomato juice

Combine the celery salt, horseradish, lemon juice, orange juice, Worcestershire sauce, salt, sugar and tomato juice in a large bowl. Process 1/4 at a time in a blender. Combine in a pitcher and stir to mix well. Chill, covered, for 8 hours. Serve in chilled glasses.

Serves 6 to 8

MALIBU BERRY

1/3 cup Malibu rum
1/3 cup framboise liqueur
2/3 cup piña colada mix
2 cups ice

Combine the rum, raspberry liqueur, piña colada mix and ice in a blender and process until smooth. Serve in chilled glasses.

Serves 2

HELPFUL HINT

Make a delicious Tropical Infusion beverage by pouring two 20-ounce cans of undrained pineapple chunks into a large pitcher; top with 20 ounces of vodka and let stand, covered, for 24 hours or longer. Pour 2 ounces of the infusion into a shaker. Add ice and shake. Pour the mixture into a martini glass and enjoy.

OKLAHOMA SUNRISE

HELPFUL HINT

Stirring the punch gently when adding the Champagne helps to retain its bubbles.

1 (12-ounce) can frozen orange juice concentrate, thawed
1 (12-ounce) can apricot nectar, chilled
3 cups water
1 1/2 pints strawberry or raspberry sorbet, softened
1 (750-milliliter) bottle Champagne, chilled
3 cups crushed ice
strawberries

Prepare the orange juice concentrate as directed on the package. Combine the prepared orange juice, apricot nectar and water in a large glass container. Chill, covered, for 1 hour or longer. Spoon the sorbet into a large punch bowl. Pour the orange juice mixture over the sorbet. Add the Champagne and ice and mix gently. Serve in stemmed glasses and garnish with whole strawberries.

Makes 1 gallon

COFFEE PUNCH

4 quarts brewed strong coffee
6 cinnamon sticks
2/3 cup sugar
4 cups whipping cream, whipped
2 quarts vanilla ice cream, softened

Combine the hot coffee, cinnamon sticks and sugar in a 1-gallon container and stir to blend. Chill, covered, for 8 to 10 hours.

Combine the coffee mixture with the whipped cream and ice cream in a large punch bowl at serving time. Mix gently.

Serves 60

CRUNCHY PUNCH

3 (3-ounce) packages strawberry gelatin
9 cups boiling water
4 cups each water and sugar
1 (16-ounce) bottle lemon juice
2 (46-ounce) cans pineapple juice
2 large bottles ginger ale

Combine the gelatin in the boiling water in a large bowl, stirring to dissolve completely. Combine 4 cups water and sugar in a medium saucepan and mix well. Bring to a boil over high heat and cook until the sugar dissolves, stirring constantly. Remove from heat and let stand until cool.

Pour the cooled sugar mixture into the gelatin mixture and mix well. Add the lemon juice and pineapple juice and mix well. Pour into several small plastic freezer containers or sealable plastic freezer bags and seal. Freeze for several hours.

Thaw the mixture in the containers for 30 minutes before serving time. Spoon the partially frozen mixture into a large punch bowl and add the ginger ale, mashing with a large fork or potato masher until the punch is slushy and of the desired consistency.

Serves 15 to 20

BIG AL'S YOGURT SMOOTHEE

1/2 cup orange juice
1/4 cup yogurt
1 banana, peeled, sliced, frozen
1 tablespoon honey

Combine the orange juice, yogurt, banana and honey in a blender and blend until smooth and thick. The juice and yogurt give this drink a tart taste.

Serves 1

BRUNCH BREADS

Ailene Martin's Best-Ever Cheese Soufflé

HELPFUL HINT

Prepare a Creamy Dip for fresh fruit by whipping 1 cup whipping cream in a blender; add 8 ounces softened cream cheese, 1 1/2 cups confectioners' sugar and 1 teaspoon vanilla extract and blend until thick and of the desired consistency. Serve with fresh whole strawberries or chunks of fresh fruit for dipping. This refreshing cold dip is excellent for a brunch or shower.

1 tablespoon shredded Swiss cheese
3 tablespoons butter
3 tablespoons flour
1 cup hot milk
4 egg yolks
salt, pepper and nutmeg to taste
5 egg whites
1/2 teaspoon salt
3/4 cup shredded sharp Cheddar cheese

Sprinkle the Swiss cheese in a buttered 1 1/2-quart soufflé dish. Melt the 3 tablespoons butter in a small saucepan over low heat and add the flour, stirring to combine. Cook until bubbly. Cook for 2 minutes longer, stirring constantly; do not brown. Remove from the heat and beat in the hot milk.

Cook for 1 minute or until very thick, stirring constantly. Remove from the heat and beat in the egg yolks 1 at a time. Season with salt, pepper and nutmeg to taste.

Beat the egg whites with 1/2 teaspoon salt in a small bowl until stiff peaks form. Stir 1 spoonful of the egg whites into the egg yolk mixture. Fold in the Cheddar cheese and remaining egg whites gently.

Preheat the oven to 400 degrees. Pour the soufflé mixture into the prepared dish and place the dish in a larger baking pan. Fill the baking pan halfway up the side of the soufflé dish with hot water. Place the pan in the oven and reduce the oven temperature to 350 degrees. Bake for 40 minutes or until puffed and golden brown. Serve immediately.

Serves 4

BREAKFAST SAUSAGE PATTIES

8 ounces ground turkey
8 ounces mild Italian sausage, casings removed
1/4 cup finely chopped red onion
2 tablespoons finely chopped celery
2 tablespoons finely chopped fennel
2 tablespoons finely chopped yellow bell pepper
2 garlic cloves, minced
1 tablespoon minced Italian parsley
2 teaspoons minced fresh thyme
1/4 teaspoon fennel seeds, crushed
1/2 teaspoon salt
1/2 teaspoon pepper

Combine the ground turkey, sausage, red onion, celery, fennel, bell pepper, garlic, parsley, thyme, fennel seeds, salt and pepper in a large bowl and mix well. Chill, covered, for 8 hours or longer.

Divide sausage mixture into 16 equal portions. Shape each portion into a ball and flatten into patties 1/3 inch thick. Cook the patties in a preheated large nonstick sauté pan over medium-low heat for 1 to 2 minutes or until brown on the bottom. Turn the patties and cook for 1 to 2 minutes longer or until brown. Cover the pan and turn off the heat. Let stand for 5 minutes to continue to cook through. Drain the patties on paper towels and serve warm.

Serves 8

HELPFUL HINT

To core and slice fennel, trim the stalks close to the bulb, discarding the bruised outer stalks. Cut the bulb lengthwise into halves or quarters and rinse between the layers to remove any grit. Remove and discard the core from each piece. Slice as needed for use in recipes.

Cowboy Chiles Rellenos

HELPFUL HINT

Rellenos are stuffed green chiles that are deep-fried. In the Southwest, they are usually filled with cheese. In some parts of Mexico, dried as well as fresh chiles are sometimes stuffed with picadillo, a savory meat filling, to make rellenos.

2 (4-ounce) cans whole green chiles, drained
2 cups shredded Cheddar cheese
2 cups shredded Monterey Jack cheese
2 eggs, beaten
2 tablespoons flour
1/4 cup milk
1/2 cup sour cream
1/4 teaspoon pepper
1/8 teaspoon salt

Cut the chiles into halves lengthwise and discard the seeds. Arrange 1/3 of the chiles in a round 8-inch baking dish. Mix the cheeses in a small bowl. Sprinkle 1/3 of the cheese mixture over the chiles. Layer the remaining chiles and cheese 1/2 at a time in the prepared dish.

Combine the eggs, flour, milk, sour cream, pepper and salt in a small bowl and whisk until smooth. Pour the mixture over the layers in the baking dish. Let stand for 30 minutes or chill, covered, until needed.

Bake at 350 degrees for 30 to 40 minutes or until brown and bubbly. Cool on a wire rack for 20 minutes. Serve with Western Potatoes (page 45).

You may double this recipe and bake in a 3-quart baking dish for 40 to 50 minutes.

Serves 3 or 4

WESTERN POTATOES

6 medium potatoes, baked
1 tablespoon (heaping) chopped red bell pepper
1 tablespoon (heaping) chopped green bell pepper
1 tablespoon minced chives
salt and pepper to taste
1 tablespoon Worcestershire sauce
3 tablespoons heavy cream
1/2 cup (1 stick) butter

Chop the unpeeled baked potatoes into small pieces. Combine the potatoes, bell peppers, chives, salt and pepper in a large bowl and mix well. Add the Worcestershire sauce and cream and mix lightly.

Melt the butter in a large skillet over medium-high heat and heat until hot. Shape the potato mixture into patties and cook in the hot butter for 7 minutes or until brown on the bottom. Turn the potato cakes and cook until brown. Arrange the potato cakes on a platter and serve warm.

Serves 6 to 8

ROLLED SMOKED SALMON FRITTATA

1 tablespoon olive oil
6 eggs, beaten
1/3 cup cream cheese, softened
1/2 medium red onion, thinly sliced

3 tablespoons capers
3 to 4 ounces smoked salmon,
   in pieces

Heat the olive oil in a large nonstick sauté pan over low heat. Add the eggs and cook, covered, just until the eggs are set; do not stir or overcook. Remove the frittata carefully to a sheet of plastic wrap and cool.

Spread the cream cheese evenly over the cooled frittata. Sprinkle evenly with the onion, capers and salmon. Roll the frittata as tightly as possible to enclose the filling, taking care not to tear the eggs. Wrap tightly in plastic wrap and chill for 30 minutes or longer.

Unwrap the frittata and place it on a serving platter. Cut into 1/4- to 1/2-inch slices, discarding the ends. Serve with sliced prosciutto, fruit or toasted bagel pieces.

Serves 4 to 6

BAKED EGGS ON CREAMED SPINACH

12 ounces fresh spinach, rinsed,
   stemmed
salt to taste
2 tablespoons minced onion
1 tablespoon unsalted butter

3 tablespoons heavy cream
freshly grated nutmeg to taste
pepper to taste
2 eggs

Cook the spinach in salted boiling water in a 2- to 3-quart saucepan over high heat for 2 minutes. Drain in a sieve, pressing out the excess moisture with the back of a large spoon; chop finely.

Sauté the onion in the butter in a small nonstick skillet over medium-low heat until tender, stirring frequently. Stir in the spinach, cream, nutmeg, salt and pepper. Cook until heated through, stirring constantly.

Spoon into two 1/3- to 1/2-cup buttered ramekins and break 1 egg into each ramekin. Arrange the ramekins on a baking sheet. Bake at 400 degrees in the upper third of the oven for 12 minutes or until the egg whites are cooked through and the yolks are done to taste. Adjust the seasoning and serve immediately.

Serves 2

Photograph for this recipe appears on page 40.

SPINACH EGG PUFF

1 (10-ounce) package frozen chopped spinach, thawed
10 eggs
1/2 cup flour
1/2 teaspoon salt
1 teaspoon baking powder
16 ounces cottage cheese
16 ounces shredded cheese
1/2 cup (1 stick) butter, melted

HELPFUL HINT

For a Chile Egg Puff, substitute 3 chopped scallions, 1/2 chopped mild green chile and 1 cup cooked corn kernels for the spinach. Serve with salsa.

Drain the spinach, pressing out the excess moisture. Beat the eggs in a large bowl until thick and pale yellow. Add the spinach, flour, salt, baking powder, cottage cheese, cheese and butter and mix well. Spoon into a buttered 9×13-inch baking pan. Bake at 350 degrees for 35 minutes or until set and golden brown.

Serves 12 to 14

MARKET TOMATO PIE

1 (1-crust) pie pastry
1/4 cup grated Parmesan cheese
4 medium tomatoes, sliced
1/2 cup chopped onion
salt and pepper to taste
3/4 cup mayonnaise
2 cups shredded mozzarella cheese
1/4 cup grated Parmesan cheese

Line a 9-inch pie plate with the pie pastry and flute the edge. Sprinkle evenly with 1/4 cup Parmesan cheese. Bake at 350 degrees for 5 minutes. Layer the tomatoes, onion and salt and pepper to taste 1/2 at a time over the pastry. Combine the mayonnaise and mozzarella cheese in a small bowl and mix well. Spoon over the layers. Sprinkle with 1/4 cup Parmesan cheese. Bake at 350 degrees for 30 minutes or until the top is brown.

You may substitute squash or chopped spinach for the tomatoes in this recipe.

Serves 6   *Photograph for this recipe appears on page 40.*

Rice Torte in Cheddar Fennel Crust

Cheddar Fennel Crust
1 1/4 cups flour
1/2 teaspoon salt
1/2 teaspoon crushed fennel seeds

1/2 cup (1 stick) butter, softened
3/4 cup shredded sharp Cheddar
  cheese, softened

Torte
8 slices bacon
1 cup thinly sliced zucchini
1 cup thinly sliced yellow squash
1/2 cup finely chopped yellow onion
2 large garlic cloves, minced
1/2 teaspoon thyme

6 eggs, beaten
1 cup sour cream
1 teaspoon salt
2 cups cooked arborio rice
1 cup shredded Cheddar cheese

For the crust, combine the flour, salt and fennel seeds in a food processor and pulse once or twice to mix well. Add the butter and cheese and process until the mixture forms a ball of dough. Pat the dough evenly over the bottom and 1 inch up the side of an 8- or 9-inch springform pan and set aside.

For the torte, cook the bacon in a large skillet over medium heat until crisp. Drain and crumble the bacon; set aside. Drain the skillet, reserving 2 tablespoons of the bacon drippings. Heat the reserved drippings in the skillet over medium heat and add the zucchini, yellow squash, onion, garlic and thyme to the skillet. Cook for 10 minutes or until the vegetables are tender, stirring occasionally.

Combine the eggs, sour cream, salt, rice, cheese, squash mixture and bacon in a large bowl and mix well. Pour into the pastry-lined pan and smooth the top with a spatula. Bake at 350 degrees for 55 minutes or until golden brown and set. Cool on a wire rack for 15 minutes or longer. Loosen the edge from the side of the pan with a knife and remove the side of the pan. Cut into wedges and serve warm or cold.

Serves 12

POPOVERS

2 eggs, beaten
1 cup milk
1 cup flour, sifted
1/2 teaspoon salt

Beat the eggs with the milk in a medium bowl. Add the flour and salt and mix well. Spoon into buttered muffin cups, filling halfway. Bake at 475 degrees for 15 minutes. Reduce the oven temperature to 350 degrees and bake for 30 minutes longer without opening the oven door.

Serves 8

STRAWBERRY BUTTER

1/2 cup (1 stick) butter, softened
1/2 cup puréed fresh strawberries
1 teaspoon lemon juice
1/2 teaspoon confectioners' sugar

Combine the butter, strawberries, lemon juice and confectioners' sugar in a small bowl and mix until smooth and creamy. Serve at room temperature. Store, covered, in the refrigerator.

You may substitute strawberry jam for the fresh strawberries when they are out of season.

Makes about 1 cup

BUTTER PECAN PANCAKES

1/2 cup chopped pecans
3 tablespoons lemon juice
2 tablespoons sugar
1 3/4 cups flour
1 1/2 teaspoons baking powder
1 teaspoon baking soda
1 teaspoon salt
2 eggs, beaten
2 cups buttermilk
1/4 cup (1/2 stick) butter, melted

Combine the pecans, lemon juice and sugar in a small skillet and heat over medium heat until the sugar melts and coats the pecans, stirring constantly. Remove from the heat and set aside.

Sift the flour, baking powder, baking soda and salt into a medium bowl. Add the eggs and buttermilk and mix until well blended. Stir in the pecan mixture and butter gently; the batter should be lumpy.

Pour the batter 1/4 cup at a time onto a hot lightly greased griddle. Cook until bubbles appear on the surface and the underside is golden brown. Turn the pancake and cook until golden brown.

Serves 6

Tulsa French Toast

1/2 baguette, cut into 1-inch slices
6 eggs
1 1/2 cups milk
1 cup light cream or half-and-half
1 teaspoon vanilla extract
1/4 teaspoon cinnamon
1/4 teaspoon nutmeg
1/4 cup (1/2 stick) butter, melted
1/2 cup packed brown sugar
1 tablespoon light corn syrup
1/2 cup chopped nuts

Arrange the baguette slices in a single overlapping layer in a buttered 9×13-inch baking dish. Combine the eggs, milk, cream, vanilla, cinnamon and nutmeg in a large bowl and beat until well blended. Pour over the baguette slices. Chill, covered, for 8 hours or longer.

Combine the butter, brown sugar, corn syrup and nuts in a small bowl and mix well. Spread the mixture over the chilled baguette slices. Bake at 350 degrees for 40 minutes. Serve warm with maple syrup.

Serves 6

In 1929, the Ambassador Hotel was established. It was an extended-stay hotel for oil barons and their families while their mansions were being built. The hotel, located in downtown Tulsa, recently underwent major renovation and is listed on the National Registry of Historic Places.

Wonderful Waffles

4 egg yolks
2 cups heavy cream
2 cups sifted flour
2 teaspoons baking powder
1 teaspoon salt
1 tablespoon sugar
1/4 cup (1/2 stick) butter or margarine, melted
4 egg whites
milk

Beat the egg yolks in a large bowl until thick and pale yellow. Add the cream and mix just until blended. Sift the flour, baking powder, salt and sugar together. Add the sifted dry ingredients to the egg yolk mixture all at once and stir just until combined. Blend in the butter just until smooth.

Beat the egg whites in a small bowl until stiff peaks form. Fold into the batter gently. Thin the batter if needed with enough milk to make of the desired consistency.

Cook in a waffle iron using the manufacturer's instructions. Serve with melted butter, warm maple syrup and fresh fruit.

Serves 6

APRICOT AND PRUNE COFFEE CAKE

STREUSEL MIXTURE
1/2 cup packed brown sugar
2 tablespoons flour
1 teaspoon cinnamon
2 tablespoons butter

COFFEE CAKE
3/4 cup chopped dried apricots
3/4 cup chopped prunes
3/4 cup (1 1/2 sticks) butter, softened
1 1/2 cups sugar
4 eggs
1 1/2 teaspoons vanilla extract
3 cups flour
1 1/2 teaspoons baking powder
3/4 teaspoon baking soda
1/4 teaspoon salt
1 cup sour cream
2 tablespoons confectioners' sugar

HELPFUL HINT

Chop dried prunes and dried apricots with a sharp knife or kitchen shears. To prevent the knife or shears from becoming sticky, dip the blades frequently in hot water or spray them lightly with cooking spray.

TO PREPARE THE STRUESEL MIXTURE, combine the brown sugar, flour and cinnamon in a small bowl. Cut in the butter until the mixture is crumbly.

TO PREPARE THE COFFEE CAKE, mix the dried fruit together and set aside. Cream the butter and sugar in a large bowl until light and fluffy. Beat in the eggs 1 at a time. Add the vanilla and mix well.

Sift the flour, baking powder, baking soda and salt together. Add the sifted dry ingredients to the creamed mixture alternately with the sour cream, beating just until smooth after each addition. Fold in the dried fruit mixture.

Alternate layers of the batter and streusel mixture one-third at a time in a greased and floured 10-inch tube pan. Bake at 350 degrees for 55 to 60 minutes or until the coffee cake tests done. Cool in the pan on a wire rack for 20 minutes. Remove from the pan and sift the confectioners' sugar over the top of the coffee cake.

Serves 16

GINGERBREAD

GINGERBREAD
1/4 cup (1/2 stick) butter, softened
1/4 cup sugar
1 egg, beaten
1/2 cup light corn syrup
1 cup flour

1/2 teaspoon ginger
1/2 teaspoon allspice
1/2 teaspoon baking soda
1 teaspoon baking powder
1/4 cup milk

GINGERBREAD SAUCE
1/4 cup (1/2 stick) butter, softened
1 cup packed brown sugar
2 egg yolks, beaten

1/2 cup milk
2 egg whites, stiffly beaten

FOR THE GINGERBREAD, cream the butter and sugar in a medium bowl until light and fluffy. Add the egg and corn syrup and mix well. Sift the flour, ginger, allspice, baking soda and baking powder together. Add the sifted dry ingredients to the creamed mixture alternately with the milk, mixing well after each addition.

Pour into a greased 8×8-inch baking pan. Bake at 350 degrees for 20 to 30 minutes or until the gingerbread tests done. Remove to a wire rack to cool.

FOR THE SAUCE, cream the butter and brown sugar in a medium bowl until light and fluffy. Add the egg yolks and the milk and beat until smooth. Pour into a heavy saucepan and cook over medium heat until thickened, stirring constantly. Fold into the beaten egg whites. Serve with the warm gingerbread. Store, covered, in the refrigerator. Reheat before serving.

Serves 4 to 6

BLUEBERRY AND ALMOND COTTAGE BREAD

2 cups flour
1 tablespoon baking powder
1/4 teaspoon salt
3/4 cup sugar
2 eggs
1/4 cup (1/2 stick) butter, melted, cooled
1 cup milk
1 teaspoon almond extract
1/2 cup slivered almonds
11/2 cups fresh or frozen blueberries, drained

HELPFUL HINT

Fresh blueberries are in season only from June through August and should be used within one week of purchase.

Mix the flour, baking powder, salt and sugar in a bowl. Beat the eggs with the butter, milk and almond extract in a bowl. Make a well in the center of the flour mixture and add the egg mixture and the almonds, stirring just until mixed. Fold in the blueberries.

Pour into a greased and floured 5×9-inch loaf pan. Bake at 350 degrees for 1 hour or until golden brown and a tester inserted in the center comes out clean; the top of the bread will crack. Cool on a wire rack for 10 minutes. Loosen from the edges of the pan and remove to a wire rack to cool completely. Serve warm.

Serves 10 to 12

CRANBERRY NUT BREAD

HELPFUL HINT

Fresh cranberries are available in stores from autumn through the holiday season. They should be used within one week of purchase or frozen for up to three months.

$1/2$ cup (1 stick) butter, softened
1 cup sugar
2 eggs
1 teaspoon vanilla extract
2 cups flour
1 teaspoon baking soda
$1/4$ teaspoon salt
$2/3$ cup buttermilk
1 cup chopped fresh cranberries
$1/2$ cup chopped walnuts

Cream the butter and sugar in a mixing bowl until light and fluffy. Add the eggs and vanilla and beat well. Sift the flour, baking soda and salt together. Add the sifted dry ingredients to the creamed mixture alternately with the buttermilk, mixing well after each addition. Stir in the cranberries and walnuts.

Spoon the batter into 3 greased 16-ounce cans. Bake at 350 degrees for 45 to 50 minutes or until a wooden pick inserted in the bread comes out clean. Cool in the cans for 5 minutes. Remove to a wire rack to cool completely.

Serves 12 to 18

STILWELL STRAWBERRY BREAD

2 (10-ounce) packages frozen sliced strawberries, thawed
3 cups flour
2 cups sugar
1 teaspoon salt
1 teaspoon baking soda
1/2 teaspoon cinnamon
4 eggs, beaten
1 cup corn oil
6 ounces cream cheese, softened

HELPFUL HINT

Stilwell, Oklahoma, is the strawberry capital of Oklahoma and has hosted a strawberry festival each May since 1947.

Drain the strawberries, reserving the juice. Sift the flour, sugar, salt, baking soda and cinnamon into a bowl. Combine the eggs, oil and strawberries in a medium bowl and mix well. Make a well in the center of the flour mixture. Add the egg mixture and mix thoroughly but gently.

Line 3 loaf pans with greased foil. Spoon the batter into the pans. Bake at 325 degrees for 1 hour or until the loaves test done. Cool the loaves on a wire rack. Wrap each loaf in foil and refrigerate for 24 hours before serving.

Combine the cream cheese and reserved strawberry juice in a medium bowl and beat until thick and pink. Serve with the bread.

Makes 3 loaves

BLUEBERRY MUFFINS

1/2 cup (1 stick) butter, softened
1 1/4 cups sugar
2 eggs
2 cups flour
2 teaspoons baking powder
1/2 teaspoon salt
1/2 cup milk
1/2 cup fresh blueberries, mashed
2 cups fresh blueberries
2 teaspoons sugar

Cream the butter and 1 1/4 cups sugar at low speed in a mixing bowl until light and fluffy. Add the eggs 1 at a time, beating after each addition. Sift the flour, baking powder and salt together. Add the sifted dry ingredients to the creamed mixture alternately with the milk, mixing well after each addition. Stir in the mashed blueberries and fold in the whole blueberries.

Grease a 12-cup muffin pan, including the top of the pan. Spoon the batter evenly into the prepared muffin cups. Sprinkle evenly with 2 teaspoons sugar. Bake at 375 degrees for 25 to 30 minutes or until the muffins test done. Cool in the pan for 30 minutes or longer.

Makes 1 dozen

MACADAMIA NUT MUFFINS

1/2 cup (1 stick) unsalted butter, softened
1 cup packed light brown sugar
3 eggs
3/4 teaspoon almond extract
1/2 teaspoon vanilla extract
1 cup plus 2 tablespoons bread flour
1 1/4 teaspoons baking powder
1/2 teaspoon salt
1/4 cup heavy cream
3/4 cup coarsely chopped macadamia nuts
1/3 cup whole macadamia nuts

Cream the butter and brown sugar in a mixing bowl until
light and fluffy. Beat in the eggs. Add the flavorings and beat
until smooth.

Sift the flour, baking powder and salt together. Add to the creamed
mixture and mix well. Add the cream and beat just until smooth.
Fold in the chopped macadamia nuts.

Spoon the batter into 10 paper-lined muffin cups. Sprinkle with
the whole macadamia nuts. Bake at 350 degrees for 25 minutes
or until a tester inserted in the center of a muffin comes out clean.
Remove to a wire rack to cool. Serve the muffins warm or at
room temperature.

Makes 10

*William Skelly,
founder of Skelly
Oil Company, died in
1957. His chauffeur,
Morris Jolly, placed
a flower on his grave
every week for more
than ten years.*

ORANGE MUFFINS

3/4 cup flour
3/4 cup plus 3 tablespoons bran
1/2 cup sugar
1 teaspoon baking soda
1 teaspoon baking powder
1 teaspoon cinnamon
1/2 cup raisins
1 unpeeled navel orange, cut into eighths
1/2 cup orange juice
1/2 cup molasses
1 egg
1/4 cup (1/2 stick) margarine, melted

Combine the flour, bran, sugar, baking soda, baking powder, cinnamon and raisins in a bowl and mix well. Purée the orange pieces and orange juice in a blender. Add the molasses, egg and margarine and blend until well mixed. Add to the dry ingredients and stir just until mixed.

Spoon into 18 greased large muffin cups. Bake at 425 degrees for 15 minutes or until the muffins test done. Cool in the pans for 10 minutes and remove to a wire rack to cool completely.

Makes 18

CORN MUFFINS WITH GREEN ONIONS AND SOUR CREAM

1 cup unbleached flour
1 cup yellow cornmeal
$^1/_4$ cup sugar
2 teaspoons baking powder
$1^1/_2$ teaspoons salt
$^1/_2$ teaspoon baking soda
$^1/_2$ teaspoon pepper
1 cup sour cream
2 eggs
$^1/_4$ cup ($^1/_2$ stick) unsalted butter, melted, cooled
$1^1/_2$ cups frozen corn kernels, thawed, drained
1 cup chopped green onions

Combine the flour, cornmeal, sugar, baking powder, salt, baking soda and pepper in a bowl and mix well. Whisk the sour cream, eggs and butter in a small bowl. Add to the dry ingredients and stir just until mixed. Fold in the corn and green onions.

Spoon the batter evenly into 12 paper-lined $^1/_3$-cup muffin cups. Bake at 425 degrees for 20 minutes or until golden brown and a tester inserted in the center of a muffin comes out clean. Cool on a wire rack.

These muffins are a great accompaniment to the Cowboy Chiles Rellenos on page 44.

Makes 1 dozen

Lavinia's Cinnamon Rolls

Brown Sugar Filling
1 cup packed brown sugar
1 cup sugar
2 tablespoons cinnamon

Rolls
2 cakes yeast
1/2 cup sugar
2 cups milk, scalded, cooled to lukewarm
6 to 7 cups flour
2 teaspoons salt
1/2 cup shortening, melted, cooled
2 eggs, beaten
1 cup (2 sticks) butter, softened
1 3/4 cups sugar
1 1/4 cups honey or corn syrup

For the filling, combine the brown sugar, sugar and cinnamon in a medium bowl and mix well.

For the rolls, dissolve the yeast and 1/2 cup sugar in the lukewarm milk in a large bowl. Add 3 cups of the flour and the salt and beat until smooth. Add the shortening and eggs and mix well. Add enough of the remaining 3 to 4 cups flour to make a dough that is easily workable.

Knead on a floured surface for 10 minutes or until smooth and elastic. Place in a greased bowl, turning to coat the surface. Let rise, covered, in a warm place until doubled in bulk.

Roll into a 1/4-inch-thick rectangle on a lightly floured surface.

Spread the dough evenly with one-fourth to one-half of the butter. Sprinkle with the filling. Roll to enclose the filling and cut into 1-inch slices.

Spoon the remaining butter, sugar and honey into 30 muffin cups. Arrange the dough slices in the prepared muffin cups. Let rise until the centers puff. Bake at 350 degrees for 10 to 12 minutes or until brown.

Makes 30

COUNCIL OAK CREAM CHEESE BRAID

SOUR CREAM DOUGH
1 cup sour cream
1/2 cup sugar
1 teaspoon salt
1/2 cup (1 stick) butter, melted

2 envelopes dry yeast
1/2 cup warm water
2 eggs
4 cups flour

CREAM CHEESE FILLING
16 ounces cream cheese, softened
3/4 cup sugar
1 egg

1/8 teaspoon salt
2 teaspoons vanilla extract

VANILLA GLAZE
2 cups confectioners' sugar
1/4 cup milk

2 teaspoons vanilla extract

FOR THE DOUGH, heat the sour cream in a small saucepan over low heat. Stir in the sugar, salt and butter. Cool to lukewarm. Sprinkle the yeast over the warm water in a large mixing bowl and mix until the yeast dissolves. Add the sour cream mixture, eggs and flour and mix well to make a dough. Chill, tightly covered, for 8 hours or longer.

FOR THE FILLING, combine the cream cheese and sugar in a bowl and mix well. Add the egg, salt and vanilla and mix well.

Divide the dough into 4 equal portions. Roll each portion into an 8×12-inch rectangle on a floured surface. Spread each rectangle evenly with one-fourth of the filling. Roll each as for a jelly roll, starting with a long edge and sealing the edge and ends.

Place seam side down on greased baking sheets. Slice 2/3 of the way through each loaf with a knife at 2-inch intervals to create a braided appearance. Let rise, covered, in a warm place for 1 hour or until doubled in bulk. Bake at 375 degrees for 12 to 15 minutes or until golden brown.

FOR THE GLAZE, combine the confectioners' sugar, milk and vanilla in a bowl and mix well. Spread over the warm loaves.

Serves 15 to 20

DELICIOUS DILL BREAD

1 envelope dry yeast
$1/4$ cup warm water
1 cup cottage cheese
2 teaspoons dillseeds
1 teaspoon salt
$1/4$ teaspoon baking soda
1 tablespoon dried minced onion
2 tablespoons sugar
1 tablespoon butter, softened
1 egg
$2^{1}/2$ cups flour, sifted

Dissolve the yeast in the warm water. Combine the cottage cheese, dillseeds, salt, baking soda, onion, sugar, butter and egg in a large bowl and mix well. Add the yeast mixture and stir to mix well. Add the flour gradually, mixing well after each addition.

Let rise in a warm place for 50 minutes. Punch the dough down and place in a greased $1^{1}/2$-quart baking dish. Let rise for 30 to 40 minutes. Bake at 350 degrees for 40 to 50 minutes or until golden brown.

Serves 8

MARY'S DINNER ROLLS

3/4 cup shortening
2/3 cup sugar
1 cup boiling water
2 egg whites
2 envelopes dry yeast
1 cup warm water
5 1/2 cups flour
1 teaspoon salt
1/2 cup (1 stick) butter, melted

Combine the shortening, sugar and boiling water in a small bowl and mix well. Set aside to cool. Beat the egg whites in a small bowl until stiff peaks form.

Dissolve the yeast in the warm water in a large mixing bowl. Add 1 cup of the flour and the salt to the yeast mixture and mix well. Add the remaining flour 1 cup at a time, mixing well after each addition. Add the egg whites to the yeast mixture alternately with the cooled shortening mixture, mixing well after each addition.

Place in a greased bowl, turning to coat the surface. Chill, covered with foil, for 2 hours or longer. Let rise, covered, in a warm place for 2 hours.

Roll the dough to a 1/2-inch thickness on a floured surface. Shape into dinner rolls and arrange on a greased baking sheet. Let rise for 2 hours. Brush the tops with the butter. Bake at 375 degrees for 10 to 12 minutes. Cool on a wire rack.

Makes 4 dozen

HELPFUL HINT

For Mary's Cinnamon Rolls, start with the recipe for Mary's Dinner Rolls and sprinkle the rolled dough with a mixture of 2 teaspoons cinnamon, 1/2 cup sugar and 1/2 cup chopped nuts. Roll as for a jelly roll and cut into 1-inch slices. Arrange on a greased baking sheet and proceed as for Dinner Rolls.

HERBED TOMATO FOCACCIA

6 garlic cloves, minced
3/4 teaspoon crushed dried red pepper
3/4 cup olive oil
1 envelope dry yeast
2 cups warm (105- to 115-degree) water
5 cups (about) unbleached flour
2 teaspoons salt
8 medium Roma tomatoes, seeded, cut into 1-inch pieces
2 tablespoons coarse salt
2 tablespoons chopped fresh rosemary
2 tablespoons thinly sliced fresh basil

Sauté the garlic with the red pepper in the olive oil in a small heavy saucepan over medium-low heat for 5 minutes or until the garlic is golden brown, stirring constantly. Remove from the heat and let stand for 1 hour or longer.

Sprinkle the yeast over the warm water in a large glass measuring cup and let stand for 10 minutes or until the yeast is dissolved. Whisk in 3 tablespoons of the oil from the garlic mixture.

Combine 2 cups of the flour and 2 teaspoons salt in a large mixing bowl. Add the yeast mixture and beat until well blended. Beat in enough of the remaining flour 1 cup at a time to form a soft dough. Beat at low speed for 3 minutes or until the dough is smooth.

Brush a large bowl with 1 tablespoon of the oil from the garlic mixture. Place the dough in the prepared bowl, turning to coat the surface. Let rise, covered with plastic wrap and a damp kitchen towel, in a warm place for 1 hour or until doubled in bulk.

Toss the tomatoes with 1 tablespoon of the coarse salt in a colander set over a large bowl. Let stand for 15 minutes. Rinse the tomatoes with cold water and drain on paper towels.

Brush a 10×15-inch baking pan with 1 tablespoon of the oil from the garlic mixture. Punch the dough down and knead briefly in the bowl. Place the dough on the prepared pan and stretch the dough to fit the pan with oiled hands. Dimple the dough evenly by pressing with fingertips. Sprinkle evenly with the rosemary, tomatoes, basil and remaining 1 tablespoon coarse salt.

Bake at 450 degrees for 30 minutes or until golden brown. Remove to a wire rack to cool. Cut into squares and serve with the remaining oil from the garlic mixture. Serve with grilled meat.

Serves 10 to 12

ONION AND FENNEL FLATBREAD

1/4 cup (1/2 stick) unsalted butter
1 1/2 cups finely chopped onion
1 cup warm (105- to 115-degree) water
1 envelope quick-rising yeast
1 teaspoon sugar
1 1/4 teaspoons salt
2 teaspoons fennel seeds, crushed
3 cups (about) flour
2 teaspoons unsalted butter, softened
2 teaspoons fennel seeds

Melt 1/4 cup butter in a medium heavy saucepan over medium-low heat. Add the onion and sauté for 15 minutes or until very tender, stirring frequently. Place the mixture in the large bowl of an electric mixer fitted with a dough hook. Add the warm water, yeast, sugar, salt and crushed fennel seeds and mix well. Add enough of the flour 1/2 cup at a time to make a medium-soft dough. Knead on a floured surface for 4 minutes or until smooth and elastic.

Let rise, covered with a towel, on the work surface for 20 minutes or until dough begins to rise. Knead the dough briefly and divide into 4 equal portions. Shape each portion into a ball and flatten each into a 5-inch circle 3/4 inch thick. Arrange the circles on a buttered 10×15-inch baking sheet and rub the tops with 2 teaspoons butter.

Sprinkle the whole fennel seeds evenly over the tops and press gently so the seeds adhere. Let rise, covered with a towel, in a warm place for 30 minutes or until puffed. Bake at 425 degrees for 25 minutes or until golden brown. Serve warm.

Makes 4 round loaves

SALADS

GRAPEVINE SALAD

BALSAMIC VINAIGRETTE DRESSING
1/4 cup balsamic vinegar
1/2 teaspoon oregano
1/8 teaspoon pepper
1/4 teaspoon salt
1/2 cup olive oil or vegetable oil
1 tablespoon sugar

SALAD
2 cups sliced seedless red grapes
1/2 cup crumbled Gorgonzola cheese
1/2 cup chopped walnuts
romaine leaves

TO PREPARE THE DRESSING, combine the vinegar, oregano, pepper, salt, olive oil and sugar in a tightly covered jar and shake to blend.

TO PREPARE THE SALAD, combine the grapes, cheese and walnuts in a medium bowl and mix gently. Spoon onto salad plates. Shape each to resemble a bunch of grapes. Arrange the romaine leaves at the top to resemble the grape leaves. Drizzle the dressing over the top of each salad. Serve immediately.

Serves 4

Beef Salad with Asparagus and Broccoli

FLANK STEAK SALAD
1 small flank steak
salt to taste
4 cups 2-inch diagonally sliced pieces fresh asparagus
1 bunch broccoli, cut into bite-size florets

GINGER DRESSING
1/3 cup light soy sauce
1/4 cup white vinegar
3 tablespoons sesame oil
1 (1 1/2-inch) piece fresh gingerroot, grated
1 teaspoon sugar
freshly ground white pepper to taste

TO PREPARE THE SALAD, grill, broil or pan-fry the flank steak for 5 minutes on each side or until done to taste. Cool and thinly slice the steak on the diagonal.

Bring enough salted water to cover the asparagus to a boil in a medium saucepan over high heat. Add the asparagus and cook for 30 seconds. Remove with a slotted spoon and set aside to cool. Add the broccoli to the boiling water and cook for 30 seconds. Drain and set aside to cool.

TO PREPARE THE DRESSING, combine the soy sauce, vinegar, sesame oil, gingerroot, sugar and white pepper in a small bowl and whisk until well blended.

To serve, toss the steak slices with the dressing in a medium bowl. Add the asparagus and broccoli and toss. Arrange the salad on a platter lined with green leaf lettuce. Serve at room temperature.

Serves 4

HEARTS OF PALM AND PROSCIUTTO SALAD

HELPFUL HINT

*Hearts of palm
come from the
stem of the
cabbage palm tree,
which grows in
wetland conditions,
primarily in South
America. The
slightly tart flavor
of the delicious
hearts of palm
pairs well with
both the flavors
and colors of the
prosciutto and
the thyme in this
salad.*

2 (14-ounce) cans hearts of palm, drained
8 ounces prosciutto, thinly sliced
1/4 cup white wine vinegar
1/2 cup olive oil
1/2 teaspoon thyme
1/4 teaspoon pepper
1 garlic clove, crushed
Boston lettuce or curly endive

Cut the hearts of palm lengthwise into quarters or thirds. Wrap each piece in a small slice of the prosciutto and secure with a wooden pick. Place the wrapped slices in a shallow glass dish.

Whisk the vinegar, olive oil, thyme, pepper and garlic in a small bowl and pour over the top. Chill, covered, for 8 hours or longer; drain. Line 6 salad plates with the lettuce and arrange the wrapped hearts of palm over the top. Serve at room temperature.

This recipe makes an excellent first course for a dinner party.

Serves 6

Asian Chicken and Spinach Salad with Cashews

Garlic and Sesame Marinade
2 tablespoons soy sauce
1 tablespoon sesame oil

1 teaspoon minced garlic
1 tablespoon chopped scallions

Salad
4 boneless skinless chicken breasts
2 packages fresh spinach, rinsed, stemmed
1 head Napa cabbage, thinly sliced
1 medium red bell pepper, thinly sliced

1 cup shiitake mushrooms, sliced
1/2 cup julienned carrots
1/2 cup bean sprouts
1/2 cup whole cashews
1/4 cup chopped green onions

Ginger Sesame Dressing
1/4 cup rice vinegar
1/4 cup soy sauce
2 tablespoons sesame oil
1/4 cup peanut oil

2 teaspoons dry mustard
2 teaspoons sesame seeds, toasted
2 teaspoons minced garlic
2 teaspoons grated fresh gingerroot

TO PREPARE THE MARINADE, whisk the soy sauce, sesame oil, garlic and scallions in a small bowl.

TO PREPARE THE SALAD, arrange the chicken in a shallow nonreactive dish. Pour the marinade over the chicken and refrigerate, covered, for 1 hour or longer. Drain and discard the marinade.

Preheat the oven to 350 degrees. Heat a nonstick ovenproof skillet over high heat until hot. Add the chicken and sear over high heat on both sides until brown. Bake for 10 minutes or until the chicken is cooked through. Cool and slice into thin strips.

Combine the chicken, spinach, cabbage, bell pepper, mushrooms, carrots, bean sprouts, cashews and green onions in a large salad bowl and toss lightly.

TO PREPARE THE DRESSING, combine the vinegar, soy sauce, sesame oil, peanut oil, dry mustard, sesame seeds, garlic and gingerroot in a small bowl and whisk until well blended.

To serve, pour the dressing over the salad and toss gently. Serve from the salad bowl or on individual dinner plates. Garnish with crisply fried won tons and toasted sesame seeds.

Serves 4

Chicken and Wild Rice Salad

Helpful Hint

Fresh apricots, pitted and sliced, may be substituted for the seedless grapes in this recipe when they are in season, from late June to early August.

Tarragon Dressing
1 shallot, chopped
3 garlic cloves, minced
1/4 cup tarragon vinegar
1/4 cup white wine
1 teaspoon light soy sauce
1 tablespoon almond oil or safflower oil
1 tablespoon vegetable oil
freshly cracked pepper to taste
2 tablespoons chopped fresh tarragon

Salad
9 cups torn butter lettuce leaves (about 3 heads)
3 cups cooked wild rice
2 cups red or green seedless grapes, cut into halves
1 cup shredded cooked chicken
1 cup chopped celery
1/2 cup toasted walnuts
1/4 cup minced parsley
1/4 cup chopped chives
12 large butter lettuce leaves

To prepare the dressing, combine the shallot, garlic, vinegar, wine and soy sauce in a blender and blend until mixed. Add the oils in a fine stream, blending constantly at high speed until smooth. Add the pepper and tarragon and blend just until mixed.

To prepare the salad, combine the lettuce, wild rice, grapes, chicken, celery, walnuts, parsley and chives in a large salad bowl and toss lightly. Chill, covered, until ready to serve.

Pour the dressing over the salad and mix gently. Spoon onto 12 lettuce-lined salad plates.

Serves 12　　　　　*Photograph for this recipe appears on page 68.*

TAIPEI CHICKEN WITH MIXED GREENS

2 cups warm shredded cooked chicken
1 cup crisp chow mein noodles
1/4 cup thinly sliced green onions
1/4 cup soy sauce
2 tablespoons sesame oil
2 tablespoons rice vinegar
2 tablespoons water
2 teaspoons sugar
2 teaspoons grated fresh gingerroot
1 tablespoon chopped seeded red or green jalapeño chile
4 cups mixed salad greens

Combine the warm chicken, chow mein noodles and green onions in a medium bowl and mix gently. Combine the soy sauce, sesame oil, vinegar, water, sugar, gingerroot and jalapeño in a small saucepan and mix well. Bring to a boil over medium-high heat, stirring constantly until the sugar dissolves. Remove from the heat and pour over the chicken mixture; toss gently to mix.

Arrange the salad greens on a platter and spoon the chicken mixture onto the greens. Serve immediately.

Serves 4

RED SNAPPER SALAD

2 medium tomatoes, cored, cut into thin wedges
3 tablespoons chopped red onion
2 tablespoons thinly sliced fresh basil, or 2 teaspoons dried basil
1 tablespoon chopped fresh dill, or 1 teaspoon dried dillweed
1 tablespoon chopped fresh mint
1 tablespoon olive oil
1 large garlic clove, minced
salt and pepper to taste
4 (5- to 6-ounce) red snapper fillets

Combine the tomatoes, onion, basil, dill, mint, olive oil and garlic in a medium bowl and mix well. Season with salt and pepper and set aside.

Place each snapper fillet in the center of a sheet of foil large enough to enclose the fish; sprinkle the fish with salt and pepper. Spoon one-fourth of the tomato salad over each fillet. Fold the foil tightly to enclose the fish and salad and seal tightly.

Grill the packets seam side up over medium-high heat or broil 6 inches from the heat source for 12 minutes or until the fish is cooked through and the salad is warm. Serve packets on individual plates and allow guests to open their own packets.

Serves 4

SHRIMP AND RICE SALAD FLORENTINE

12 ounces large fresh shrimp, cooked, peeled, deveined
1 cup uncooked long grain rice
1 (8-ounce) bottle wine-flavor vinaigrette salad dressing
1 tablespoon teriyaki sauce
1 teaspoon sugar
2 cups thinly sliced fresh spinach
1/2 cup sliced celery
1/2 cup sliced green onions
1/3 cup crumbled crisp-fried bacon (about 6 slices)
1 (8-ounce) can sliced water chestnuts, drained

Cut each shrimp into halves. Cook the rice according to the package directions. Combine the hot rice and shrimp in a large bowl and let cool slightly.

Whisk the salad dressing, teriyaki sauce and sugar in a small bowl. Pour over the rice mixture and toss to mix well. Chill, covered, until serving time.

Add the spinach, celery, green onions, bacon and water chestnuts to the rice mixture and mix gently.

Serves 6 to 8

TILAPIA AND ROMAINE SALAD

GARLIC VINAIGRETTE
1 garlic clove, cut into halves
3 tablespoons extra-virgin olive oil
1 tablespoon white wine vinegar

1/2 teaspoon salt
1/4 teaspoon pepper
1/2 teaspoon dry mustard

SALAD
1 head romaine, shredded
1 cup seasoned croutons
1/2 cup crumbled bleu cheese
1/4 cup grated Parmesan cheese

6 small tilapia fillets
flour for coating
salt and pepper
olive oil

TO PREPARE THE VINAIGRETTE, rub the interior surface of a wooden salad bowl with the cut sides of the garlic halves. Combine the olive oil, vinegar, salt, pepper and dry mustard in a small bowl and whisk until smooth. Add the garlic halves and set aside.

TO PREPARE THE SALAD, combine the lettuce, croutons and cheeses in the prepared wooden bowl and toss. Spoon onto 6 small salad plates.

Dust the fillets with flour and sprinkle with salt and pepper. Sauté the fillets in olive oil in a skillet over medium-high heat until opaque and done to taste.

Place 1 fillet on top of each salad. Remove the garlic halves from the vinaigrette and discard. Drizzle the vinaigrette over the salads.

Serves 6

ASPARAGUS WITH HAZELNUTS AND TARRAGON VINAIGRETTE

TARRAGON VINAIGRETTE
1/4 cup minced shallots
3 tablespoons tarragon white wine vinegar
4 teaspoons chopped fresh tarragon, or 1 1/4 teaspoons dried tarragon
1 teaspoon Dijon mustard
7 tablespoons hazelnut oil, walnut oil or olive oil
salt and pepper to taste

SALAD
1/4 cup hazelnuts, toasted
1 pound fresh asparagus, trimmed
4 cups baby lettuce or inner leaves of curly endive

TO PREPARE THE VINAIGRETTE, combine the shallots, vinegar, tarragon and Dijon mustard in a small bowl and mix well. Add the hazelnut oil in a fine stream, whisking until well blended. Season with salt and pepper.

FOR THE SALAD, arrange the warm toasted hazelnuts in a single layer in a kitchen towel. Fold the towel over and rub vigorously until the bitter brown skins are removed. Chop the hazelnuts coarsely and set aside.

Bring 1 inch of water to a boil in a large saucepan over high heat and insert a steamer rack. Arrange the asparagus in the rack and steam, covered, for 4 minutes or until tender-crisp. Remove the asparagus to a bowl of ice water to halt the cooking process. Drain on paper towels.

Arrange the lettuce on a large platter and place the asparagus over the top. Drizzle with the vinaigrette and sprinkle with the hazelnuts.

The asparagus salad can also be served with Creamy Mushroom Dressing (page 89), Sesame Vinaigrette (page 91) and Roasted Yellow Bell Pepper Sauce (page 116).

Serves 4

ATOMIC SALAD

3 (or more) large garlic cloves, minced
1/4 teaspoon (or more) dry mustard
1 teaspoon salt
1/2 teaspoon pepper
2 tablespoons lemon juice
2 tablespoons grated Parmesan cheese
1/2 cup vegetable oil
fresh spinach leaves, rinsed, stemmed
mixture of 2 types of fresh lettuce leaves
cherry tomatoes or tomato wedges
croutons

Combine the garlic, dry mustard, salt, pepper, lemon juice, cheese and vegetable oil in a large salad bowl and whisk until well blended. Adjust the garlic or dry mustard for a spicier flavor.

Arrange the desired amount of spinach and lettuce over the top of the dressing; do not mix. Chill, covered, for 8 hours or until ready to serve. Add the tomatoes and croutons at serving time and toss to mix well.

Serves 4 to 8

GOLDEN DRILLER SALAD

DRILLER DRESSING
1/3 cup red wine vinegar
1/4 cup olive oil
1 teaspoon sugar
salt and pepper to taste
1 garlic clove

SALAD
2 (15-ounce) cans black beans, rinsed, drained
1 (10-ounce) package frozen corn, thawed
1 avocado, coarsely chopped
1 red bell pepper, chopped
1 red onion, chopped
1 bunch fresh cilantro, chopped
1/4 teaspoon chili powder
16 ounces Monterey Jack cheese, cut into cubes

TO PREPARE THE DRESSING, combine the vinegar, olive oil, sugar and salt and pepper to taste in a small bowl and whisk until well blended. Add the garlic clove and let stand for 30 minutes.

TO PREPARE THE SALAD, combine the beans, corn, avocado, bell pepper, onion, cilantro, chili powder and cheese in a large salad bowl and mix well.

Remove and discard the garlic clove from the dressing. Pour the dressing over the salad, tossing to mix well. Serve with tortilla chips.

Serves 8

The Golden Driller is Tulsa's own 76-foot-high helmeted oil field worker, towering over an oil derrick. Erected in 1966 to commemorate Tulsa's tenure as the Oil Capital of the World, he is supported by 2 1/2 miles of rod and mesh and is the largest freestanding statue in the world.

Blackened Portobello Salad

Mustard Marinade

1/4 cup red wine vinegar
1/4 cup balsamic vinegar
1/4 cup tomato juice
1 tablespoon olive oil
2 teaspoons Dijon mustard
2 teaspoons stone-ground mustard
1/4 teaspoon coarsely ground pepper

Salad

4 (4-ounce) portobello mushroom caps, each about 5 inches in diameter
1 tablespoon Cajun steak seasoning
2 teaspoons olive oil
16 cups mixed gourmet salad greens
1 large tomato, cut into 8 wedges
1/2 cup thinly sliced red onion, separated into rings
1 (15-ounce) can cannellini or other white beans, rinsed, drained
1/4 cup crumbled bleu cheese

To prepare the marinade, combine the vinegars, tomato juice, olive oil, mustards and pepper in a sealable plastic bag and seal the bag, kneading to mix.

To prepare the salad, add the mushrooms to the marinade and seal the bag. Marinate for 10 minutes, turning the bag occasionally. Remove the mushrooms, reserving the marinade.

Sprinkle the mushrooms with the Cajun seasoning. Heat the olive oil in a large nonstick skillet sprayed with cooking spray over medium-high heat until hot. Add the mushrooms and cook for 2 minutes on each side or until very brown. Cool and cut into thin diagonal slices.

Divide the salad greens evenly among 4 plates. Top each with one-fourth of the mushroom slices, tomato wedges and onion rings. Sprinkle each salad with one-fourth of the beans and 1 tablespoon of the bleu cheese. Drizzle with the reserved marinade.

Serves 4

CHÈVRE SALAD WITH HOT CIDER DRESSING

HOT CIDER DRESSING
2 cups apple cider
8 slices bacon, cut into 1-inch pieces
3 shallots, minced
1 teaspoon cinnamon
1 tablespoon honey mustard
1/2 cup olive oil
2 tablespoons wine vinegar
salt and freshly ground pepper to taste

SALAD
12 cups torn mixed salad greens, such as leaf lettuce, radicchio,
    endive or watercress
1 cup Spiced Pecans (at right)
1 cup thinly sliced fennel
1 1/2 large McIntosh apples, cored, thinly sliced
4 ounces crumbled Montrachet cheese or other
    chèvre cheese

TO PREPARE THE DRESSING, bring the cider to a boil in a small saucepan over medium heat. Cook for 20 to 25 minutes or until reduced to 1/2 cup; set aside.

Fry the bacon in a medium skillet over medium-high heat until crisp. Drain on paper towels and crumble, reserving for the salad. Drain the skillet, reserving 3 tablespoons of the drippings in the skillet. Add the shallots to the drippings and sauté over medium heat for 3 minutes or until tender, stirring frequently. Whisk in the cinnamon and honey mustard and cook for 1 minute.

Add the reduced cider, olive oil, vinegar and salt and pepper to taste and mix well. Keep the dressing hot over medium-low heat.

TO PREPARE THE SALAD, toss the greens with 1 cup of the Spiced Pecans, reserved bacon, fennel, apples and cheese in a large salad bowl. Pour the dressing over the salad and toss to coat. Serve immediately.

Serves 6

HELPFUL HINT

Make Spiced Pecans by combining 2 cups pecan halves with boiling water and soaking for 15 minutes; drain and pat dry. Spread in a single layer on an ungreased baking sheet. Toast at 300 degrees for 45 minutes, stirring occasionally. Whisk together 2 1/2 tablespoons vegetable oil, 1/4 cup sugar, 1 teaspoon each salt and cinnamon, 1/2 teaspoon each ginger and dry mustard and 1/4 teaspoon each nutmeg and ground cloves. Add the pecans and stir to coat well. Spread on the same baking sheet and roast at 350 degrees for 15 minutes. Cool and store in an airtight container for up to 2 weeks.

GRILLED SUMMER SALAD

HELPFUL HINT

*Many paper
bags now contain
recycled elements
that can become a
health hazard
when heated. If a
safe paper bag is
unavailable, or if
you are unsure
of the bag's
content, simply
place the roasted
vegetables in a
covered saucepan
to steam. This
process will loosen
the charred skins
for peeling just as
well as steaming
the vegetables in a
paper bag, and
cleanup is a breeze.*

GRILLED VEGETABLES
6 to 8 fresh poblano chiles
6 Roma tomatoes (about 2 pounds)
2 medium green bell peppers
2 medium red bell peppers
8 garlic cloves, unpeeled

CUMIN AND CORIANDER DRESSING
1/4 cup olive oil
3 tablespoons fresh lemon juice
3/4 teaspoon salt
1/2 teaspoon cumin
coriander to taste
freshly ground pepper to taste
anise to taste
1 tablespoon tiny capers (optional)

TO GRILL THE VEGETABLES, arrange the poblanos, tomatoes, bell peppers and garlic on a greased rack. Grill over medium-high heat or broil 5 inches from the heat source until the vegetable skins crack and char. Place the charred vegetables in a paper bag or covered bowl and let cool for 10 minutes.

Peel, seed and coarsely chop the poblanos, tomatoes and bell peppers. Peel and mash the garlic. Combine the poblanos, tomatoes, bell peppers and garlic in a nonreactive salad bowl and toss. Let stand for 1 hour or longer to allow the flavors to blend.

TO PREPARE THE DRESSING, combine the olive oil, lemon juice, salt, cumin, coriander, pepper, anise and capers in a small bowl and whisk until well mixed. Pour over the salad and toss to coat well.

The salad may be prepared up to 1 day in advance and stored in the refrigerator. Let stand at room temperature for 30 minutes before adding the dressing and tossing to serve.

Serves 8 to 10

Mandarin Orange Salad

Salad
1 head iceberg lettuce, torn into bite-size pieces
1 head romaine, torn into bite-size pieces
1 small purple onion, thinly sliced, separated into rings
1 (8-ounce) can mandarin oranges, drained
1 (2^1/2-ounce) package sliced almonds, toasted

Mustard Vinaigrette
1 cup vegetable oil
^{1}/2 cup tarragon wine vinegar
1 tablespoon sugar
1 teaspoon tarragon
^{1}/2 teaspoon Dijon mustard
^{1}/2 teaspoon salt
^{1}/4 teaspoon white pepper

TO PREPARE THE SALAD, combine the lettuces, onion, mandarin oranges and almonds in a large salad bowl and toss.

TO PREPARE THE VINAIGRETTE, combine the vegetable oil, vinegar, sugar, tarragon, Dijon mustard, salt and pepper in a blender and blend for 30 seconds or until smooth. Pour over the salad and toss to coat.

Serves 10

LEBANESE LEMON SALAD

1 small head lettuce, coarsely chopped
2 large tomatoes, coarsely chopped
1/2 bunch green onions, chopped
1 cup fresh parsley, chopped
1 garlic clove
1 teaspoon salt
juice of 1 lemon
1/3 cup vegetable oil
4 sprigs of mint

Combine the lettuce, tomatoes, green onions and parsley in a medium salad bowl and toss lightly. Mash the garlic with the salt in a small bowl. Stir in the lemon juice. Add to the salad and toss to combine. Pour the vegetable oil over the salad and toss to coat. Top with the mint sprigs.

Serves 6

BACKYARD TOMATOES

HELPFUL HINT

Tomatoes ripen nicely on a sunny windowsill, usually in a day or two. They should always be stored at room temperature rather than in the refrigerator.

2/3 cup vegetable oil
1/4 cup red wine vinegar
1/4 cup parsley, chopped
1/4 cup chopped green onions with tops
1 garlic clove, minced
1 teaspoon salt
1 teaspoon dillweed
1 teaspoon basil
1/4 teaspoon pepper
4 medium tomatoes, peeled

Combine the vegetable oil, vinegar, parsley, green onions, garlic, salt, dillweed, basil and pepper in a small bowl or tightly covered jar and whisk or shake until well mixed. Cut the tomatoes into 1/2-inch-thick slices and arrange in a serving dish. Pour the dressing over the top. Chill, covered, for 2 hours, basting occasionally.

Serves 6

Turkey Mountain Salad

ONION VINAIGRETTE
1/3 cup chopped white onion
3 tablespoons cider vinegar
2 teaspoons spicy brown mustard
1/2 teaspoon sugar
1/2 teaspoon salt
1/4 teaspoon freshly ground pepper
3/4 cup olive oil

SALAD
2 heads romaine, torn into bite-size pieces
1 (14-ounce) can artichoke hearts, drained, cut into quarters
1 large avocado, chopped
8 ounces sliced bacon, crisp-fried, crumbled
1 cup freshly grated Parmesan cheese

TO PREPARE THE VINAIGRETTE, purée the onion with the vinegar in a food processor or blender. Pour into a medium bowl and whisk in the mustard, sugar, salt and pepper. Add the olive oil in a fine stream, whisking constantly until thickened.

TO PREPARE THE SALAD, combine the lettuce, artichokes, avocado, bacon and cheese in a large salad bowl and toss. Add enough of the vinaigrette to coat the salad and toss. Serve immediately.

Serves 6

HELPFUL HINT

To test an avocado for ripeness, try to flick off the small stem. If it comes off easily and there is green underneath, the avocado is ripe. If it does not come off or if there is brown underneath the stem after prying it off, the avocado is not yet useable.

SUPER SALAD

SUPER SALAD DRESSING

1 cup vegetable oil
1/2 cup fresh lemon juice
2 tablespoons honey
1 teaspoon salt

1 teaspoon Worcestershire
   sauce
2 garlic cloves, chopped

SALAD

1 head iceberg lettuce, torn
   into bite-size pieces
1 head romaine, torn into
   bite-size pieces

3 green onions, chopped
4 large mushrooms, sliced
1/4 cup sesame seeds, toasted
1/2 cup grated Romano cheese

TO PREPARE THE DRESSING, combine the vegetable oil, lemon juice, honey, salt, Worcestershire sauce and garlic in a blender and blend until smooth.

TO PREPARE THE SALAD, combine the lettuces, green onions and mushrooms in a large salad bowl and toss. Pour the dressing over the salad and toss to coat. Sprinkle with the toasted sesame seeds and cheese.

Serves 8

BALSAMIC DRESSING

2 tablespoons olive oil
1/4 cup balsamic vinegar
1 1/2 teaspoons chopped fresh
   Italian parsley
1 1/2 teaspoons chopped fresh
   basil

2 garlic cloves, minced
1 teaspoon Dijon mustard
1/2 teaspoon honey
1 teaspoon salt
1/8 teaspoon freshly ground
   pepper

Combine the olive oil, vinegar, parsley, basil, garlic, mustard, honey, salt and pepper in a small bowl and whisk until well blended. Serve over fresh tomatoes and mozzarella cheese or toss with a fresh green salad.

Makes about 1/2 cup

BALSAMIC VINAIGRETTE

1/2 cup balsamic vinegar
3 tablespoons Dijon mustard
3 tablespoons honey
2 garlic cloves, minced
2 shallots, minced
1/4 teaspoon salt
1/8 teaspoon pepper
1 cup olive oil

Whisk the vinegar, mustard, honey, garlic, shallots, salt and pepper in a medium bowl until well blended. Add the olive oil in a fine stream, whisking constantly until well mixed.

Makes 1 2/3 cups

CREAMY MUSHROOM DRESSING

8 ounces mushrooms, very thinly sliced
3 tablespoons fresh lemon juice
salt and pepper to taste
1/2 cup heavy cream
2 tablespoons Dijon mustard
1/3 cup olive oil
1 teaspoon (heaping) chopped fresh tarragon, or 1/2 teaspoon dried tarragon

Toss the mushrooms with the lemon juice in a medium bowl and season with salt and pepper. Let stand for 30 minutes at room temperature or chill, covered, for up to 2 hours.

Whisk the cream and mustard in a small bowl until blended. Add the olive oil in a fine stream, whisking constantly until well blended. Let stand for 30 minutes at room temperature or refrigerate, covered, for up to 2 hours. Whisk in the tarragon.

Drain the mushrooms and combine them with the dressing, mixing well. Serve over steamed asparagus or substitute for the Tarragon Vinaigrette in the asparagus recipe on page 79.

Makes about 3 cups

Monkey Salad Dressing

1 1/2 cups vegetable oil
1/2 cup vinegar
6 tablespoons minced fresh parsley
3 tablespoons minced green bell pepper
1/2 teaspoon red pepper
1 large onion, chopped
1 tablespoon confectioners' sugar
1 tablespoon salt
1 teaspoon dry mustard
3 ounces cream cheese, cut into small pieces, softened

Combine the vegetable oil, vinegar, parsley, green pepper, red pepper, onion, confectioners' sugar, salt and dry mustard in a blender and process until smooth. Add the cream cheese and blend until smooth and creamy.

Makes about 3 cups

Poppy Seed Fruit Salad Dressing

1 (6-ounce) can frozen orange juice concentrate, thawed
2 teaspoons poppy seeds
3 tablespoons cornstarch
1 1/2 cups pineapple juice
1 1/4 cups sugar

Combine the orange juice concentrate, poppy seeds, cornstarch, pineapple juice and sugar in a medium saucepan and mix well. Cook over medium heat until the mixture thickens, stirring frequently. Chill, covered, until serving time. Serve over fresh fruit salad.

Makes about 3 1/2 cups

PERFECT VINAIGRETTE

1 tablespoon sugar
2 teaspoons salt
1/2 teaspoon freshly ground pepper
1/3 cup red wine vinegar
1/2 cup olive oil
1/2 cup vegetable oil
1/2 teaspoon Dijon mustard
1 garlic clove, cut into halves

Combine the sugar, salt, pepper and vinegar in a tightly covered jar. Shake until well mixed. Add the oils, mustard and garlic and shake to mix well.

Makes about 1 1/2 cups

SESAME VINAIGRETTE

8 teaspoons sesame oil
4 teaspoons rice vinegar
4 teaspoons soy sauce
1 teaspoon sugar
salt and pepper to taste

Combine the sesame oil, vinegar, soy sauce and sugar in a small bowl and mix well. Add salt and pepper to taste and whisk to blend. Serve over steamed asparagus and garnish with toasted sesame seeds. You may also substitute it for the Tarragon Vinaigrette in the asparagus recipe on page 79.

Makes about 1/3 cup

SOUPS
SANDWICHES
SAUCES

Chilled Strawberry Soup in Melon Bowls

2 pints fresh strawberries, rinsed, hulled
1 cup orange juice
1 1/4 teaspoons tapioca instant pudding mix
1/8 teaspoon allspice

1/8 teaspoon cinnamon
1/2 cup sugar
1 teaspoon grated lemon zest
1 tablespoon lemon juice
1 cup buttermilk
2 cantaloupes, chilled

Reserve 6 of the strawberries. Purée the remaining strawberries in a food processor or blender. Strain the puréed strawberries into a medium saucepan. Add the orange juice and mix well. Set aside. Combine the pudding mix and 1/4 cup of the strawberry mixture in a small bowl and mix well. Add to the remaining strawberry mixture in the saucepan with the allspice and cinnamon; mix well. Bring to a boil over medium heat, stirring constantly. Cook for 1 minute or until thickened, stirring constantly.

Remove from heat and combine with the sugar, lemon zest, lemon juice and buttermilk in a large bowl and mix well. Slice the reserved strawberries and fold into the soup. Chill, covered, for 8 hours or longer. Cut each cantaloupe into halves and discard the seeds. Remove enough of the pulp to leave a shell. Spoon the soup into the cantaloupe shells and garnish with thin lemon slices.

Serves 4

Photograph for this recipe appears on page 92.

Spring Broccoli Soup

1 bunch broccoli, cut into florets
salt to taste
3/4 cup chopped onion
1/4 cup (1/2 stick) butter
2 tablespoons flour
2 cups chicken broth

1 1/2 teaspoons Worcestershire sauce
1 1/2 teaspoons Tabasco sauce
3/4 teaspoon salt
2 cups milk
1 cup shredded sharp cheese
1/4 cup chopped fresh parsley

Cook the broccoli in salted boiling water to cover in a medium saucepan over medium-high heat until tender; drain. Sauté the onion in the butter in a large saucepan over medium heat until tender. Sprinkle with the flour and cook until bubbly, stirring constantly. Add the chicken broth gradually, stirring constantly. Bring the mixture to a boil over medium-low heat, stirring constantly. Reduce the heat and add the Worcestershire sauce, Tabasco sauce, 3/4 teaspoon salt, broccoli and milk and mix well. Add the cheese and cook until the cheese melts. Heat to serving temperature. Sprinkle servings with the parsley.

Serves 4 to 6

CHICKEN À LA RHINE SOUP

1/4 cup (1/2 stick) butter
1/4 cup flour
4 cups chicken broth
2 cups half-and-half
1/4 cup (1/2 stick) butter
1/2 cup chopped onion
1/2 cup chopped celery
1/4 cup chopped green bell pepper
1/4 cup chopped red bell pepper
2 cups chopped cooked chicken
1 cup cooked rice
1/4 cup sherry
1 tablespoon Worcestershire sauce

Melt 1/4 cup butter in a large saucepan and stir in the flour. Cook over medium heat until thick and golden brown, stirring constantly. Add the chicken broth and bring to a boil over high heat, stirring constantly. Cook until the mixture is smooth and thick, stirring constantly. Remove from the heat and strain if necessary to remove any lumps. Blend in the half-and-half.

Melt 1/4 cup butter in a medium skillet over medium heat. Add the onion, celery and bell peppers and sauté over medium-high heat until the vegetables are tender, stirring constantly. Add to the soup.

Add the chicken, rice, sherry and Worcestershire sauce and stir to combine. Heat to serving temperature.

Serves 6 to 8

Spicy Chicken Chowder

Helpful Hint

Poblano chile peppers, called ancho chiles when they are dried, are cone-shaped with a long tip. They have a very shiny green or red skin and medium heat.

1 1/2 cups (3 sticks) unsalted butter
1 1/2 cups flour
3 tablespoons olive oil
1 pound carrots, peeled, chopped
1 pound onions, chopped
1 bunch celery, trimmed, sliced
3 tablespoons minced garlic
9 to 10 ounces poblano chiles, seeded, chopped
1 tablespoon (or more) cumin
1/2 bunch cilantro, minced
3/4 cup chicken broth
1 teaspoon (or more) white pepper
3 tablespoons hot red pepper sauce
heavy cream
1 cup warm chopped cooked chicken

Melt the butter in a medium saucepan over medium heat. Add the flour and cook for 4 to 5 minutes or until smooth and thick but not brown, stirring frequently. Remove from the heat and set aside.

Heat the olive oil in a large saucepan over medium-high heat. Add the carrots, onions, celery, garlic, poblanos, cumin and cilantro and sauté for 8 to 10 minutes or until the vegetables are slightly tender, stirring constantly. Add the chicken broth and pepper and cook for 10 to 12 minutes or until the carrots are tender-crisp, stirring occasionally.

Whisk the flour mixture into the soup and cook for 5 minutes longer, stirring frequently. Remove from the heat and add the hot red pepper sauce, stirring to mix well. Set aside to cool.

To serve, combine 2 parts of the soup mixture with 1 part heavy cream in the top of a double boiler. Add the warm chicken and heat to serving temperature. Garnish with colored tortilla strips and chopped jalapeños.

Serves 8

CHOW DOWN CHILI

2 tablespoons olive oil
2 pounds sirloin steak, cut into 1-inch cubes
8 ounces lean ground beef
12 ounces chorizo, casings removed, crumbled
1 large yellow onion, coarsely chopped
1/4 cup chili powder
1 tablespoon garlic salt
2 teaspoons cumin
1 teaspoon basil
2 (15-ounce) cans whole tomatoes
2 (15-ounce) cans beef broth
1 cup chopped fresh cilantro
1 cinnamon stick
3 bay leaves
2 green jalapeño chiles, slit lengthwise 3 times
1 tablespoon yellow cornmeal
salt and pepper to taste

HELPFUL HINT

Chorizo is a spicy, coarsely ground pork sausage flavored with garlic, chili powder, and other spices. It is widely used in traditional Mexican cooking. The chorizo sausage casing should be removed and the sausage crumbled before cooking.

Heat the olive oil in a large heavy saucepan over medium heat. Add the sirloin to the hot oil in batches to prevent overcrowding, browning on all sides and turning occasionally. Remove with a slotted spoon to a bowl. Add the ground beef, sausage and onion to the saucepan and cook until the ground beef and sausage are brown and crumbly and the onion is tender, stirring frequently; drain.

Combine the sirloin and the ground beef mixture in the saucepan and add the chili powder, garlic salt, cumin, basil and undrained tomatoes; mix well. Add the beef broth, cilantro, cinnamon stick, bay leaves, jalapeños, cornmeal, salt and pepper. Bring to a boil over medium heat, stirring frequently. Reduce the heat and simmer for 2 hours, stirring occasionally to break up the tomatoes.

Remove and discard the cinnamon stick, bay leaves and jalapeños before serving. Garnish servings with shredded cheese and sour cream.

Serves 8

GAZPACHO

8 tomatoes, chopped
2 green bell peppers, chopped
2 cucumbers, peeled, chopped
2 onions, chopped
2 garlic cloves, chopped
1/2 bunch parsley, chopped
1 cup vinegar
salt and pepper to taste
2 cups olive oil
1/4 cup bread crumbs
1 cup vegetable juice cocktail

Combine the tomatoes, bell peppers, cucumbers, onions, garlic and parsley in a nonreactive dish and mix well. Whisk the vinegar, salt and pepper in a small bowl and pour over the vegetable mixture. Marinate, covered, for 12 hours.

Pour the marinated mixture into a blender or food processor and process until finely ground. Add the olive oil, bread crumbs and vegetable juice cocktail and mix well. The soup should be of a thick consistency. Chill until serving time. Serve chilled with melba toast.

Serves 8

HOT-AND-SOUR SOUP

1/2 cup dried Chinese mushrooms
8 ounces boneless pork, trimmed, slightly frozen
1/2 cup canned bamboo shoots, rinsed, drained
2 squares Chinese bean curd, rinsed, drained
1 tablespoon soy sauce
8 cups chicken broth
1/2 teaspoon (or more) white pepper
2 tablespoons (or more) white vinegar
2 tablespoons cornstarch
3 tablespoons cold water
1 egg, lightly beaten
2 teaspoons sesame oil
1 green onion with top, thinly sliced diagonally

Soak the mushrooms in water to cover in a small bowl for 30 minutes. Drain the mushrooms, discarding any tough stems. Cut the mushrooms, pork, bamboo shoots and bean curd into uniform julienne pieces.

Combine the mushrooms, bamboo shoots, soy sauce and pork with the chicken broth in a large saucepan and mix well. Bring the mixture to a boil over medium-high heat. Reduce the heat and simmer for 3 minutes, stirring occasionally. Add the bean curd, white pepper and vinegar and bring to a boil, stirring constantly. Reduce the heat.

Combine the cornstarch and cold water in a small bowl and mix well. Add to the soup and cook until thickened, stirring constantly. Add the beaten egg gradually and cook for 1 minute, stirring gently.

Adjust the amount of white pepper and vinegar to suit individual tastes. Remove from the heat and stir in the sesame oil. Sprinkle with the chopped green onion and serve.

Serves 6 to 8

SHERRIED CREAM OF MUSHROOM SOUP

HELPFUL HINT

Sherried Cream of Mushroom Soup is good served in a bread bowl with a tossed green salad as an entrée on a winter day.

2 cups finely chopped mushrooms
1/2 cup (1 stick) butter
1/4 cup flour
1/4 teaspoon dry mustard
1 teaspoon salt
white pepper to taste
2 cups chicken broth
2 cups half-and-half
1/4 cup dry sherry
1/4 cup finely chopped chives

Sauté the mushrooms in the butter in a large heavy saucepan over medium-high heat until tender. Add the flour, mustard, salt and white pepper and cook for 1 minute, stirring constantly. Add the broth and cook until thickened, stirring constantly. Stir in the half-and-half and sherry and heat to serving temperature. Sprinkle the servings with the chives.

Serves 6

HEARTY PUMPKIN SOUP

HELPFUL HINT

Too many people miss the delicious flavor of pumpkins by using them only for decoration. Ninety-nine percent of all pumpkins sold in America are used for decoration only.

2 Granny Smith apples, peeled, cut into quarters
2 teaspoons minced garlic
1 red bell pepper, cut into quarters, seeded
1 small onion, cut into quarters
4 cups each water and chicken broth
1 (16-ounce) can pumpkin
1 cup white wine
salt and pepper to taste

Purée the apples, garlic, bell pepper and onion in a food processor. Combine with the water, broth and pumpkin in a large stockpot and mix well. Bring to a boil over medium-high heat, stirring frequently. Add the wine, salt and pepper and simmer for 15 minutes, stirring occasionally and skimming the surface as necessary. Garnish servings with a dollop of sour cream.

Serves 8 to 10

TOMATO AND ARTICHOKE SOUP

$1/2$ cup (1 stick) butter or margarine
$1 1/2$ cups finely chopped onions
$1/4$ cup packed fresh basil, chopped, or 1 teaspoon dried basil
$1/2$ teaspoon dillweed
5 cups finely chopped seeded peeled fresh tomatoes
$1/4$ cup tomato paste
$1/4$ cup flour
4 cups chicken broth
$1/2$ cup heavy cream
salt and pepper to taste
1 (14-ounce) can artichoke hearts, drained, thinly sliced
2 tablespoons butter or margarine, softened
8 ounces mozzarella cheese, shredded

Melt $1/2$ cup butter in a large heavy saucepan over medium heat. Add the onions, basil and dillweed and simmer for 15 minutes or just until the onions are translucent. Add the tomatoes and tomato paste and simmer for 30 minutes, stirring occasionally.

Combine the flour and 1 cup of the broth in a tightly covered jar and shake until well blended. Add to the saucepan with the remaining broth and mix well. Simmer for 15 minutes. Stir in the cream gradually. Season with salt and pepper and remove from the heat.

Sauté the artichokes in 2 tablespoons butter in a skillet until light brown, stirring constantly; drain.

Ladle the soup into ovenproof bowls and top with the sautéed artichokes. Place the bowls on a baking sheet and sprinkle evenly with the cheese. Broil just until the cheese melts. Garnish with croutons.

Serves 6 to 8

Tomato Basil Soup

1 (28-ounce) can crushed tomatoes
3 cups tomato juice
2 cups chicken broth
15 (or more) fresh basil leaves, chopped
1 1/2 cups heavy cream
3/4 cup (1 1/2 sticks) unsalted butter, cut into pieces
1/2 teaspoon salt
1/2 teaspoon freshly ground pepper

Combine the tomatoes, tomato juice and chicken broth in a large saucepan and simmer for 30 minutes, stirring occasionally. Stir in the basil.

Purée the soup in batches in a blender or food processor until smooth. Return the soup to the saucepan. Whisk in the cream, butter and salt and pepper. Cook over low heat until the butter is melted and the soup is heated through, whisking constantly.

Garnish servings with freshly grated Parmesan cheese and croutons. Serve in bread bowls if desired.

Serves 6 to 8

TORTILLA SOUP WITH CILANTRO AND GREEN CHILES

3 large green poblano chiles, roasted, peeled
2 tablespoons olive oil
3 garlic cloves, finely chopped
1/2 onion, chopped
1 (14-ounce) can chicken broth
1 (10-ounce) can cream of mushroom soup
1 (10-ounce) can tomatoes with green chiles
1 cup half-and-half
8 ounces Velveeta cheese, cut into large pieces
1/2 cup fresh cilantro, chopped
2 tablespoons oregano
1 cup shredded Cheddar cheese
crisp-fried flour tortilla strips

Seed and chop the roasted poblanos. Heat the olive oil in a large saucepan over medium-high heat. Add the garlic and onion and sauté until tender, stirring constantly. Add the chicken broth, chiles and cream of mushroom soup and mix well. Stir in the tomatoes with green chiles, half-and-half, Velveeta cheese, cilantro and oregano and cook until the cheese is melted, stirring frequently.

Simmer for 20 minutes over medium-low heat, stirring occasionally. Sprinkle the servings with the Cheddar cheese. Top with crisp-fried flour tortilla strips and/or chopped cooked chicken breast. Serve with a dollop of Cilantro Cumin Crème (page 114) and Guacamole (page 26).

Serves 4 to 6

HELPFUL HINT

To roast the poblano chiles, rinse the peppers and rub each one with vegetable oil. Arrange on a broiler pan or baking sheet and broil 6 inches from the heat source until the skins are cracked and charred, turning occasionally. Cool, peel and seed the peppers.

THE CHALET'S SWISS CHEESE SOUP

2 tablespoons butter
2 tablespoons flour
1/2 small onion, finely chopped
1 tablespoon butter
4 cups water
4 teaspoons chicken base
1 tablespoon (or more) white pepper
1 egg yolk
1/2 cup flour
2 cups milk
1 cup shredded Swiss cheese
3 tablespoons shredded American cheese (optional)
salt to taste
2 tablespoons chopped parsley
1 teaspoon Maggi seasoning sauce

Combine 2 tablespoons butter and 2 tablespoons flour in a small saucepan and cook over medium heat until smooth and thick; do not brown. Set aside.

Sauté the onion in 1 tablespoon butter in a large saucepan over medium-high heat until golden brown, stirring constantly. Add the water, chicken base and white pepper and mix well. Bring the mixture to a boil over high heat, stirring constantly. Reduce the heat.

Combine the egg yolk and 1/2 cup flour in a medium bowl and whisk until blended. Add the milk gradually, whisking constantly until smooth. Whisk the milk mixture into the chicken base mixture and bring to a boil, stirring constantly. Reduce the heat.

Add the cheeses and cook until melted, stirring to mix well. Whisk in the butter and flour mixture. Cook until thickened to the desired consistency, whisking constantly. Add salt and additional pepper if desired. Stir in the parsley and seasoning sauce to serve.

Serves 6

COLD CUCUMBER AND PINEAPPLE SANDWICH

1 cucumber, grated
8 ounces cream cheese, softened
1 cup drained crushed pineapple
1/2 cup finely chopped nuts
1/2 teaspoon salt
green food coloring (optional)
1 loaf thinly sliced brown bread

Drain the grated cucumber, pressing out the excess moisture. Combine the cucumber and cream cheese in a medium bowl and mix well. Mix in the pineapple and nuts. Add the salt and food coloring and mix well.

Spread evenly between the bread slices. Cut into shapes if desired and serve immediately or prepare ahead and chill, covered, until serving time.

Serves 20 *Photograph for this recipe appears on page 92.*

BAKED STUFFED CHEESE ROLLS

10 to 12 dinner rolls
8 ounces sharp Cheddar cheese, shredded
2 hard-cooked eggs, finely chopped
3 green onions with tops, finely chopped
3/4 cup (or less) vegetable oil
1 (8-ounce) can tomato sauce
3 tablespoons vinegar
1/2 teaspoon salt
1/2 teaspoon sugar
1/2 cup sliced black olives

Remove the center of each dinner roll, leaving a shell thick enough to hold its shape when stuffed. Arrange the bread shells on a nonstick baking sheet and set aside.

Combine the cheese, eggs, green onions, vegetable oil, tomato sauce, vinegar, salt, sugar and olives in a medium bowl and mix well. Spoon into the bread shells. Bake at 300 degrees for 30 minutes. Serve with soup or salad.

Serves 10 to 12

LUNCHEON LOAF

1 to 2 cucumbers, peeled, sliced
1 loaf white bread, sliced horizontally
1/2 cup (1 stick) butter, softened
egg salad prepared with 4 hard-cooked eggs
tuna salad prepared with 1 (6-ounce) can tuna
1/2 cup mayonnaise
salt to taste
2 to 3 tomatoes, peeled, sliced
8 ounces sliced bacon, crisp-fried, crumbled
10 ounces cream cheese, softened
1/4 cup half-and-half
2 teaspoons minced onion

Drain the cucumbers and pat dry with paper towels. Trim the crusts from the bread and select the 5 interior slices.

Place the bottom slice on an oblong serving platter and spread the top with one-fourth of the butter. Spread the egg salad evenly over the butter. Spread two-thirds of the remaining butter over both sides of the second bread slice and place over the egg salad. Spread evenly with the tuna salad.

Spread half of the mayonnaise over both sides of the third bread slice and place over the tuna salad. Arrange the cucumbers over the top and sprinkle lightly with salt.

Spread the remaining mayonnaise over both sides of the fourth bread slice and place over the cucumbers. Arrange the tomatoes on the bread, and sprinkle with salt and the bacon.

Spread the remaining butter over 1 side of the remaining bread slice and place the slice buttered side down over the top.

Combine the cream cheese, half-and-half and onion in a medium bowl and mix well. Spread over the top and sides of the layered loaf and chill, covered, for 1 1/2 hours or longer. Slice with a bread knife and serve with a fork. Serve with relishes and potato chips.

You may substitute chicken salad or ham salad for the tuna and egg salads.

Serves 10 to 12

PICNIC SANDWICH

DIJON VINAIGRETTE
1/2 teaspoon Dijon mustard
1 tablespoon balsamic vinegar
2 tablespoons olive oil

2 tablespoons water
salt and pepper to taste

SANDWICH
1 loaf ciabatto or Tuscan bread,
   crusts trimmed
1/2 cup tapenade
3 red bell peppers, julienned
8 ounces goat cheese, crumbled

marinated artichoke hearts, sliced
6 ounces thinly sliced prosciutto
4 ounces sliced peppered salami
chopped fresh herbs, such as
   marjoram and chervil

TO PREPARE THE VINAIGRETTE, whisk the mustard, vinegar and olive oil in a small bowl. Whisk in the water, salt and pepper.

TO PREPARE THE SANDWICH, cut the bread loaf into halves horizontally. Spread the bottom half with the tapenade and layer with the bell peppers and goat cheese. Drizzle with half the vinaigrette. Layer the artichokes, prosciutto and salami one-half at a time on the sandwich.

Drizzle with the remaining vinaigrette and sprinkle with the herbs. Top with the remaining half of the bread and wrap the sandwich tightly in plastic wrap and weight with a heavy cast-iron skillet or other heavy object to blend the flavors. Cut into long slices to serve.

Serves 6 to 8

Santa Fe Shrimp Tortilla Wrap

8 ounces (21- to 25-count) shrimp, grilled, peeled, deveined
2 cups baby lettuces
1 cup cooked black beans, drained
1 cup julienned red bell pepper
1/2 cup julienned jicama
2 medium tomatoes, coarsely chopped
2 tablespoons chopped cilantro
1 cup shredded Monterey Jack cheese
4 (10-inch) tomato jalapeño flour tortillas or flour tortillas
1/2 cup chipotle chile mayonnaise

Combine the shrimp, lettuces, beans, bell pepper, jicama, tomatoes, cilantro and cheese in a large bowl and mix well. Spread each tortilla evenly with the chipotle chile mayonnaise and spoon the shrimp mixture onto the tortillas.

Roll each tortilla tightly to enclose the filling and cut into halves on the diagonal. Arrange on a serving plate and garnish with fresh fruit.

Serves 4

SEARED SESAME-COATED SALMON SANDWICH

WASABI MAYONNAISE
1 tablespoon wasabi powder
1 tablespoon water
1/2 cup mayonnaise

SANDWICH
1 garlic clove, minced
2 teaspoons minced fresh gingerroot
2 tablespoons soy sauce
1 tablespoon rice wine vinegar
3 (6-ounce) salmon fillets
3 tablespoons sesame seeds
2 tablespoons vegetable oil
1 baguette
fresh spinach leaves
1 cucumber, thinly sliced lengthwise

HELPFUL HINT

Wasabi powder is powdered dried horseradish. It can be found in Asian markets or in the Asian section of most large supermarkets.

TO PREPARE THE MAYONNAISE, combine the wasabi powder with the water in a small bowl and stir to make a paste. Add the mayonnaise and mix well. Chill, covered, for 1 hour or longer.

TO PREPARE THE SANDWICH, combine the garlic, gingerroot, soy sauce and vinegar in a small bowl and mix well. Brush the salmon fillets with the garlic mixture and dip each fillet in the sesame seeds to coat.

Heat the vegetable oil in a nonstick skillet over medium-high heat. Add the salmon fillets and cook for 4 minutes on each side or until done to taste.

Split the baguette in half lengthwise and toast if desired. Spread the baguette halves evenly with the Wasabi Mayonnaise. Layer the bottom half with the spinach leaves, salmon fillets and cucumber slices. Top with the remaining baguette half and cut the sandwich into 4 equal portions.

Serves 4

Tulsa's largest oil field was discovered in 1905 when a gusher blew forth on land owned by a Creek Indian named Ida E. Glenn. This rich oil field was known as Glenn Pool. One of the oil wells on it produced 2,500 barrels of oil per day.

HERBED CHICKEN BURGERS

1 1/2 cups herb-seasoned stuffing mix
1 pound ground chicken
1/2 cup finely chopped celery
1/2 cup finely chopped onion
2 egg yolks
1/2 teaspoon salt
1/2 teaspoon pepper
1/2 cup chili sauce
1/2 cup whole cranberry sauce
4 large sesame seed hamburger buns

Process the stuffing mix to fine crumbs in a food processor or blender. Combine 1 cup of the crumbs with the chicken, celery, onion, egg yolks, salt and pepper in a large bowl and mix well. Divide the mixture into 4 equal portions. Shape each portion into a 3/4-inch patty.

Place the remaining crumbs in a shallow dish and dip the chicken patties in the crumbs to coat both sides.

Combine the chili sauce and cranberry sauce in a small bowl and mix well. Arrange the chicken patties on a grill rack or broiler pan brushed with vegetable oil. Grill over medium-high heat or broil 6 inches from the heat source for 7 minutes on each side or until the chicken patties are golden brown on the outside and cooked through.

Spread one-fourth of the cranberry mixture over the bottom half of each bun. Top with the chicken patties and bun tops.

Serves 4

PORTOBELLO BURGERS WITH BASIL MUSTARD SAUCE

BASIL MUSTARD SAUCE
1 cup mayonnaise
1/3 cup chopped fresh basil
2 tablespoons Dijon mustard
1 teaspoon fresh lemon juice
salt and pepper to taste

BURGERS
1/3 cup olive oil
1 tablespoon minced garlic
6 (4- to 5-inch-diameter) portobello mushroom caps
salt and pepper to taste
6 (3- to 4-inch-diameter) whole grain hamburger buns, split
6 large romaine leaves
6 large tomato slices

TO PREPARE THE SAUCE, combine the mayonnaise, basil, Dijon mustard and lemon juice in a small bowl and mix well. Season with salt and pepper and chill, covered, until ready to serve.

TO PREPARE THE BURGERS, whisk the olive oil and garlic in a small bowl. Brush the mushroom caps on both sides with the garlic mixture and season with salt and pepper.

Grill the mushrooms for 4 minutes per side or until tender and golden brown. Remove to a platter and cover with foil to keep warm. Grill the hamburger buns cut sides down for 2 minutes or until light golden brown.

To serve, layer the bottom half of each hamburger bun with 1 mushroom, 1 lettuce leaf and 1 tomato slice. Spread some of the Basil Mustard Sauce over the tomatoes and top with the remaining halves of the hamburger buns. Serve with the remaining sauce.

Serves 6

SIRLOIN BURGERS STUFFED WITH CARAMELIZED ONIONS

HELPFUL HINT

To make French Drip Beef, combine a 6- to 7-pound rump roast or well-trimmed chuck roast in a large Dutch oven with enough water to cover. Add a seasoning mixture of 1 tablespoon each cracked pepper, salt, rosemary, summer savory and oregano. Add 1 bay leaf, 1 beef bouillon cube and 1 teaspoon garlic powder. Cover and bring to a boil over high heat. Reduce the heat and simmer for 8 to 10 hours or until the roast is tender, adding more water during cooking only if necessary. Shred the meat with 2 forks and serve on rye buns or French rolls with mustard sauce. This is better prepared ahead so the flavors can meld. It also freezes well.

2 medium yellow onions, thinly sliced
2 tablespoons butter
1/3 cup extra-dry vermouth
salt and pepper to taste
1 1/2 pounds lean ground sirloin
1 cup unseasoned bread crumbs
1/4 cup steak sauce
1 teaspoon minced garlic
1 teaspoon dried Italian herbs
2 eggs
4 miniature baguettes, split

Separate the onion slices into rings and sauté in the butter in a nonstick sauté pan over medium-high heat for 7 minutes or until golden brown. Reduce the heat to medium and stir in the vermouth. Simmer until the liquid evaporates and the onions are tender, stirring occasionally. Season with salt and pepper and cool.

Combine the sirloin, bread crumbs, steak sauce, garlic, dried herbs and eggs in a large bowl and mix well. Shape the mixture into eight 3/4-inch-thick rectangles on waxed paper. Top 4 of the rectangles with the onion mixture, leaving a 1-inch border on all sides. Top with the remaining 4 rectangles and pinch the edges to enclose the onions completely.

Grill over medium-hot coals until done to taste. Place 1 sirloin burger inside each split baguette to serve.

Serves 4

CHILI SAUCE

8 quarts ripe tomatoes, peeled,
    chopped
1 quart onions, cut into quarters
1 pound celery, trimmed, cut into
    2-inch pieces
3 green bell peppers, cut into
    quarters
2 tablespoons cinnamon
1/4 teaspoon garlic salt

2 cups sugar
2 cups packed brown sugar
1 (14-ounce) bottle ketchup
1 tablespoon ground cloves
1 tablespoon dry mustard
3 tablespoons salt
2 (16-ounce) cans tomatoes
4 cups cider vinegar

Cook the chopped tomatoes in a large stockpot over medium heat until the liquid is almost evaporated, stirring occasionally. Purée the onions, celery and bell peppers in batches in a food processor.

Add the puréed vegetables, cinnamon, garlic salt, sugar, brown sugar, ketchup, ground cloves, dry mustard, salt, canned tomatoes and vinegar to the saucepot and mix well. Cook over medium-low heat for 3 hours, stirring occasionally. Cool slightly.

Pour the sauce into freezer containers and freeze or pour into sterilized jars and seal according to manufacturer's directions. Serve on hamburgers or roast beef sandwiches.

Makes 4 quarts

CHAMPAGNE MUSTARD SAUCE

1/4 cup dry mustard
1/4 cup Champagne or beer
1/4 cup honey

2 tablespoons Dijon mustard
2 tablespoons rice vinegar
1/4 teaspoon salt

Combine the dry mustard, Champagne, honey, Dijon mustard, vinegar and salt in a small saucepan and whisk until smooth. Bring to a boil over medium heat, stirring constantly. Reduce the heat to low and cook for 2 minutes or until the sauce reaches the desired consistency, stirring constantly; cool slightly. Stove, covered, in the refrigerator for up to 2 weeks. Serve warm or chilled with Asian Fusion Pork Appetizer (page 12).

Makes 1 cup

Cilantro Cumin Crème

HELPFUL HINT

Serve Cilantro Cumin Crème with roast chicken, on sandwiches, or as a garnish for the Tortilla Soup with Cilantro and Green Chiles on page 103. This intense sauce gives a high-voltage flavor kick to smoked salmon or trout.

3³/4 teaspoons cumin seeds
1 tablespoon coriander seeds
1 cup crème fraîche or sour cream
2 tablespoons heavy cream
1/2 cup coarsely chopped cilantro
2 garlic cloves, minced
3 tablespoons fresh lime juice
1 teaspoon kosher salt
1/2 teaspoon cracked pepper

Combine the cumin and coriander seeds in a small sauté pan and toast over medium heat for 5 minutes or until the seeds are aromatic and golden brown, shaking the pan frequently. Remove from the heat and cool.

Grind the seeds in a mortar with a pestle or in a spice mill. Combine the ground seeds, crème fraîche, heavy cream, cilantro, garlic, lime juice, kosher salt and pepper in a small bowl and mix well. Chill, covered, for 30 minutes or for up to 12 hours.

Makes 1 cup

Plum Lemon Sauce

1 tablespoon white sesame seeds
1/4 teaspoon finely minced garlic
1/2 teaspoon grated lemon zest
2 tablespoons lemon juice
5 tablespoons plum sauce
1/4 teaspoon Chinese chili sauce
1/8 teaspoon cinnamon

Toast the sesame seeds in a small skillet over medium heat until golden brown, stirring frequently to prevent burning. Combine the sesame seeds, garlic, lemon zest, lemon juice, plum sauce, chili sauce and cinnamon in a small bowl and mix well. Store, covered, in the refrigerator for up to 3 weeks. Serve warm or chilled with Asian Fusion Pork Appetizer (page 12).

Makes 1/2 cup

NINETEENTH-HOLE SAUCE

2 tablespoons dried onion flakes
1 tablespoon brown sugar
1 tablespoon whole mustard seeds
1 teaspoon MSG (optional)
1 teaspoon crushed dried oregano
2 teaspoons paprika
1 teaspoon chili powder
1 teaspoon cracked pepper
$1/2$ teaspoon salt
$1/2$ teaspoon ground cloves
1 bay leaf
1 garlic clove, minced
1 cup ketchup
$1/4$ cup olive oil or vegetable oil
$1/4$ cup chopped fresh tarragon
2 tablespoons wine vinegar
2 tablespoons Worcestershire sauce
2 or 3 drops of liquid smoke
$1/2$ cup water

Combine the onion, brown sugar, mustard seeds, MSG, oregano, paprika, chili powder, pepper, salt, ground cloves, bay leaf, garlic, ketchup, olive oil, tarragon, vinegar, Worcestershire sauce, liquid smoke and water in a small saucepan and mix well. Simmer over low heat for 20 to 25 minutes or until of the desired consistency. Remove the bay leaf. Store, covered, in the refrigerator. Serve with pork, round steak or eggs.

Makes about 2$1/4$ cups

ROASTED YELLOW BELL PEPPER SAUCE

2 large yellow bell peppers
1/4 cup olive oil
1 tablespoon fresh lemon juice
salt and pepper to taste

Roast the bell peppers over a gas flame or broil until the skins crack and char, turning to roast evenly. Place in a nonrecycled paper bag and let stand for 10 minutes. Peel, seed and chop the bell peppers.

Combine the chopped bell peppers and olive oil in a blender and purée until smooth. Add the lemon juice and blend until smooth. Season with salt and pepper. Drizzle over steamed asparagus and serve with any remaining sauce. You may also substitute it for the Tarragon Vinaigrette in the asparagus recipe on page 79.

Serves 8

PEANUT SAUCE

1/2 cup soy sauce
1/2 cup creamy peanut butter
1/2 cup rice vinegar
1/4 cup sesame oil
2 tablespoons sugar
2 tablespoons hot chili oil

Combine the soy sauce, peanut butter, vinegar, sesame oil, sugar and chili oil in a blender and blend until smooth.

Toss the sauce with 1 pound hot cooked linguini and garnish with sliced green onions, chopped peanuts and chopped cilantro to serve.

Makes about 2 cups

THAI DIPPING SAUCE

7 1/2 teaspoons water
2 tablespoons fish sauce
2 tablespoons lime juice
2 teaspoons honey
1/2 teaspoon Chinese chili sauce
1 garlic clove, minced
1 tablespoon thinly sliced fresh basil or mint
2 teaspoons grated fresh gingerroot

Mix the water, fish sauce, lime juice, honey, chili sauce, garlic, basil and gingerroot in a small bowl. Store, covered, in the refrigerator for up to 1 week. Serve at room temperature with the Asian Fusion Pork Appetizer (page 12).

Makes 1/2 cup

MAUI FRUIT SALSA

2 tomatoes, seeded, chopped
8 Roma tomatoes, seeded, chopped
1/2 purple onion, chopped
1/2 bunch cilantro, minced
2 tomatillos, finely chopped
1 to 2 jalapeño chiles, finely chopped
juice of 1 large lemon
salt and pepper to taste
1 papaya, chopped
1 mango, chopped
1 guava, chopped
2 avocados, chopped

HELPFUL HINT

Serve Maui Fruit Salsa over baked or grilled sea bass, halibut, or any other mild white fish.

Combine the tomatoes, onion, cilantro, tomatillos, jalapeños, lemon juice, salt and pepper in a large bowl and mix well. Combine the papaya, mango and guava in a large bowl and toss gently.

Combine the tomato mixture with the fruit mixture in a bowl and toss gently just before serving. Add the avocados and mix gently.

Serves 6 to 8

CRANBERRY SALSA

1 (15-ounce) can pineapple tidbits, drained
1/2 cup chopped fresh cranberries
3 green onions, chopped
1 1/2 tablespoons honey
1 teaspoon lemon juice
1 1/4 teaspoons minced fresh gingerroot
1/4 teaspoon ground red pepper

Combine the pineapple, cranberries, green onions, honey, lemon juice, gingerroot and red pepper in a medium bowl and mix well. Chill, covered, for 1 hour or longer before serving. Serve with ham or turkey.

Makes 1 1/2 cups

BRANDIED CRANBERRY SAUCE

4 cups fresh cranberries, rinsed, sorted
2 heaping cups (or more) sugar
1/4 cup brandy or Cognac

Place the cranberries in a shallow baking pan. Sprinkle evenly with the sugar and cover the pan tightly with double sheets of foil. Bake at 350 degrees for 1 hour; cool.

Add the brandy and sprinkle lightly with additional sugar, mixing well. Cool to room temperature and store, covered, in the refrigerator.

Makes about 2 cups

Chocolate Sauce

2 (1-ounce) squares chocolate
1/4 cup (1/2 stick) butter
2 tablespoons water
1 egg, beaten
1 cup confectioners' sugar
1 teaspoon vanilla extract

Melt the chocolate and butter in the top of a double boiler over medium-low heat. Cook until melted and smooth, stirring constantly. Stir in the water.

Combine the egg and confectioners' sugar in a small bowl and mix well. Add to the chocolate mixture and cook for 3 minutes, stirring constantly. Remove from heat and stir in the vanilla.

Makes about 1 cup

Raisin Sauce

1 1/2 cups packed light brown sugar
3 1/2 teaspoons cornstarch
2 cups water
2 tablespoons white vinegar
2 cups raisins
2 tablespoons butter
1/2 teaspoon salt
pepper to taste
1/2 teaspoon Worcestershire sauce
10 whole cloves

Mix the brown sugar and cornstarch in a large saucepan. Add the water gradually, stirring constantly until the mixture is smooth. Stir in the vinegar, raisins, butter, salt, pepper, Worcestershire sauce and cloves.

Cook over medium heat until the raisins are plump and the mixture is thick, stirring frequently. Serve hot over ham loaf or sliced ham.

Makes about 3 cups

ENTREES

BLACK-TIE CHUCK ROAST

BLACK-TIE MARINADE
2 garlic cloves, minced
2 tablespoons vegetable oil
1/2 cup red wine vinegar
1/3 cup ketchup

1 tablespoon Worcestershire sauce
1 teaspoon sugar
1 teaspoon basil, crushed

ROAST
1 (3-pound) beef chuck roast,
    1 1/2 to 2 inches thick
1 (4-ounce) can sliced mushrooms,
    drained

1/4 cup 1/4-inch slices green onions
1/4 cup sliced black olives

TO PREPARE THE MARINADE, sauté the garlic in the vegetable oil in a small saucepan over medium heat until tender but not brown, stirring constantly. Remove from heat and stir in the vinegar, ketchup, Worcestershire sauce, sugar and basil.

TO PREPARE THE ROAST, cut slashes in the fat around the edge at 1-inch intervals. Place the roast in a sealable plastic bag and pour the marinade over the roast. Seal the bag and place in a shallow pan. Marinate in the refrigerator for 1 to 2 days, turning every few hours. Drain the roast, reserving the marinade.

Grill the roast over medium coals for 25 minutes on each side for medium-rare or 30 minutes on each side for medium, brushing occasionally with the reserved marinade.

Combine the remaining reserved marinade, mushrooms, green onions and olives in a small saucepan over medium-high heat and bring to a boil, stirring constantly. Cook for 5 to 7 minutes or until heated through.

Place the roast on a platter and spoon the mushroom sauce over the top. Cut the roast across the grain into thin slices and serve with the mushroom sauce.

Serves 4 to 6

WINE SUGGESTION: *St. Joseph Rouge*

T-Town Brisket

HONEY BASTING SAUCE
1/2 cup honey
3 tablespoons soy sauce

seasoned salt to taste
Tabasco sauce to taste

BRISKET
1 (5- to 6-pound) brisket
seasoned salt to taste

1/2 to 3/4 cup sherry

DAD'S BARBECUE SAUCE
3/4 cup ketchup
1/4 cup packed brown sugar
2 tablespoons Worcestershire sauce

1/4 cup vinegar
seasoned salt to taste
Tabasco sauce to taste

TO PREPARE THE BASTING SAUCE, combine the honey, soy sauce, seasoned salt and Tabasco sauce in a small bowl and mix well; set aside.

TO PREPARE THE BRISKET, trim and discard the excess fat and place in a large covered roasting pan. Sprinkle both sides of the brisket generously with seasoned salt and add the sherry. Roast, covered, at 300 degrees for 3 hours or until easily pierced with a fork. Remove from the pan and brush with the basting sauce. Grill over low heat for 30 to 45 minutes or until done to taste.

TO PREPARE THE BARBECUE SAUCE, combine the ketchup, brown sugar, Worcestershire sauce, vinegar, seasoned salt and Tabasco sauce in a small saucepan and mix well. Cook over low heat for 15 minutes, stirring occasionally; do not boil.

Slice the brisket across the grain and serve with the barbecue sauce. Serve with Grilled Summer Salad (page 84) and Gnocchi (page 180).

Serves 8 to 12

WINE SUGGESTION: *Côtes du Rhône Red*

Roughneck Rib Roast

1 (5-pound) standing rib roast
cloves of 1 garlic bulb, minced
1 tablespoon water
1 tablespoon vegetable oil
salt and pepper to taste
12 bay leaves

Trim the layer of fat from the roast and reserve. Combine the garlic, water, vegetable oil, salt and pepper in a small bowl and mix to form a paste. Rub the entire surface of the roast with the garlic mixture and place rack side down in a roasting pan.

Arrange the bay leaves over the top of the roast and layer the reserved fat over the top, securing with kitchen string. Roast at 425 degrees for 30 minutes. Reduce the oven temperature to 250 degrees and roast for 3 hours longer without opening the oven door. Discard the bay leaves and fat.

Reserve the pan drippings to combine with 1 can of beef broth to serve the beef au jus or to use in Beef Gravy (below). Serve the roast with Mashed Potatoes with Garlic and Parmesan Cheese (page 197).

Serves 4

WINE SUGGESTION: *Full-bodied Cabernet Sauvignon*

Beef Gravy

1/4 cup beef drippings
1/4 cup flour
2 to 3 cups fresh or canned beef broth
freshly ground pepper to taste

Heat the drippings in a skillet and stir in the flour. Cook until bubbly and golden brown, stirring constantly. Add the beef broth and cook until thickened, stirring constantly. Season with pepper.

Makes 2 1/2 to 3 1/2 cups

Fabulous Fajitas

Citrus Marinade
1/2 cup soy sauce
2 1/2 cups reduced-sodium soy sauce
1 cup water
1/2 cup fresh lemon juice
1/2 cup fresh lime juice
2 tablespoons liquid smoke

4 garlic cloves, minced
1 teaspoon onion powder
1 teaspoon cayenne pepper
1 teaspoon seasoned pepper
4 teaspoons grated fresh gingerroot

Fajitas
1 skirt steak
1 large onion, thickly sliced
   vertically

1 green bell pepper, sliced
1 red bell pepper, sliced
8 flour tortillas

To prepare the marinade, combine the soy sauces, water, lemon juice, lime juice, liquid smoke, garlic, onion powder, cayenne pepper, seasoned pepper and gingerroot in a sealable plastic bag and seal the bag. Shake until well mixed and refrigerate for 24 hours to allow the flavors to blend.

To prepare the fajitas, trim and discard the fat from the steak. Place the steak in the bag with the marinade and seal the bag. Marinate for 4 to 24 hours, turning occasionally. Drain the steak, discarding the marinade.

Grill the steak over hot coals for 5 minutes on each side or until done to taste. Remove from the grill and slice into thin strips. Grill or sauté the onion and bell peppers just until tender.

To serve, spoon the steak strips, onion and bell peppers onto the tortillas and garnish with sour cream, guacamole and shredded Cheddar cheese. Wrap to enclose the filling.

This recipe won first place in a taste-off contest. The Citrus Marinade may also be used to marinate chicken tenders.

Serves 4

Beverage Suggestion: *Beer*

BEEF IN BURGUNDY

1 (5-pound) chuck roast
flour for coating
1/4 cup (1/2 stick) butter, softened
1/4 cup olive oil
salt and pepper to taste
1/4 cup Cognac
8 ounces bacon, chopped
4 garlic cloves, minced
2 carrots, sliced
2 leeks or 4 medium onions, chopped
2 tablespoons chopped parsley
2 bay leaves
1 teaspoon thyme
3 cups burgundy
1 tablespoon butter, melted
1 tablespoon flour

Cut the roast into 1-inch pieces and coat with flour. Brown the pieces in 1/4 cup butter and olive oil in a heavy skillet over high heat, turning to brown all sides. Sprinkle with salt and pepper. Add the Cognac and carefully ignite the mixture. Allow the flame to subside and remove to a baking dish.

Cook the bacon, garlic, carrots, leeks and parsley in the same skillet over medium heat until the bacon is crisp and the vegetables are light brown. Spread the vegetable mixture over the beef. Add the bay leaves, thyme, burgundy and enough water to cover. Bake, covered, at 350 degrees for 1 1/2 to 2 hours.

Combine 1 tablespoon melted butter with 1 tablespoon flour in a small bowl and stir into the beef in the baking dish. Bake for 2 to 3 hours longer or until done to taste. Serve over rice or noodles.

Serves 6 to 8

WINE SUGGESTION: *French Red Burgundy or Oregon Pinot Noir*

FIVE-STAR FLANK STEAK

1/2 cup soy sauce
1/2 cup dry white wine
1/2 cup chopped onion
3 tablespoons chopped fresh rosemary
2 tablespoons olive oil
2 garlic cloves, chopped
1/4 teaspoon coarsely ground pepper
1 (2-pound) flank steak

Combine the soy sauce, wine, onion, rosemary, olive oil, garlic
and pepper in a medium bowl and mix well. Pour into a 9×13-
inch glass dish and add the steak, turning to coat. Marinate,
covered, for 8 to 10 hours, turning occasionally.

Drain the steak, reserving the marinade in a small saucepan. Grill
the steak over high heat for 6 minutes on each side for rare or
until done to taste. Remove to a serving platter and let stand for
10 minutes.

Bring the marinade to a boil over high heat and boil for 1 minute,
stirring constantly. Cut the steak into 4 equal portions and serve
with the marinade.

Serves 4 *Photograph for this recipe appears on page 120.*

WINE SUGGESTION: *Australian Shiraz*

*In the 1920s, the
Tulsa metropolitan
area had more
millionaires per capita
than New York City.
Tulsa ruled over our
nation's oil industry for
seven decades. It was
home to many oilmen,
including Skelly,
Phillips, Cosden,
Sinclair, Getty,
Chapman, Gilcrease,
and McFarlin.*

Hungarian Beef Paprika

1 (18- to 20-ounce) round steak
2 medium onions, chopped
2 tablespoons vegetable oil
2 heaping tablespoons (or more)
    paprika

1 teaspoon salt
1 teaspoon sugar
1 (15-ounce) can sauerkraut, rinsed,
    drained (optional)

Trim and discard the fat from the steak; cut the steak into small pieces and moisten with water. Cook the onions in the vegetable oil in a Dutch oven over medium-low heat until tender, stirring occasionally. Add the paprika, steak, salt and sugar. Cook over low heat until the steak is tender, stirring occasionally and adding water as needed for the desired consistency. Add the sauerkraut and cook until heated through. Serve with sour cream.

This dish is best made a day ahead to allow the flavors to blend. Serve with light side dishes as this is a somewhat heavy dish. You may freeze the stew. You may also substitute pork for the round steak.

Serves 4 to 6

Wine Suggestion: *Any young full-bodied Red*

Bulgogi

2 pounds sirloin, partially frozen
5 green onions, chopped
4 garlic cloves, crushed
5 tablespoons soy sauce
2 tablespoons sesame oil

1/4 cup sugar
1 tablespoon sesame seeds, toasted
1/4 teaspoon pepper
peanut oil for stir-frying

Trim and discard the fat from the sirloin and cut across the grain into 1/8-inch-thick slices. Combine the green onions, garlic, soy sauce, sesame oil, sugar, sesame seeds and pepper in a sealable plastic bag and seal the bag. Shake until well mixed. Add the sirloin to the bag and seal. Marinate for 1 to 2 hours at room temperature or in the refrigerator for 8 to 10 hours; drain. Stir-fry the steak at 375 degrees in the hot peanut oil or grill over hot coals until done to taste. Serve over rice or kimchi.

Serves 6

Wine Suggestion: *Syrah*

Better-Than-Best Beef Jerky

3 pounds lean London broil, partially frozen
$^1/_2$ cup reduced-sodium soy sauce
$^1/_2$ cup reduced-sodium teriyaki sauce
2 tablespoons liquid smoke
garlic powder or granulated garlic to taste
onion powder to taste
lemon pepper and seasoned black pepper to taste
Tony Chachere's Seasoning to taste

Trim and discard the fat from the London broil and slice the beef with the grain into long $^1/_8$- to $^1/_4$-inch-wide strips. Whisk the soy sauce, teriyaki sauce, liquid smoke, garlic powder, onion powder, lemon pepper, seasoned black pepper and Tony Chachere's Seasoning in a small bowl. Combine with the beef strips in a nonreactive container or sealable plastic bag and cover the container or seal the bag. Marinate for 4 hours or longer, turning the strips or kneading the bag occasionally. Drain the beef strips and discard the marinade.

Insert a wooden pick horizontally into one end of each beef strip and sprinkle the strips with additional seasonings if desired. Place an oven rack in the highest position and hang each beef strip by its pick across two bars of the rack, staggering the placement of the beef strips to allow air circulation necessary for the drying process. Line another oven rack with foil and place it in the lowest oven position to catch any drips or spatters, leaving enough space on all four sides for air circulation. Leave the oven door ajar.

Bake at 150 to 175 degrees for 6 to 12 hours or until beef strips are dark brown, hard and dry but not burned or brittle, checking the progress after 6 hours and every hour thereafter, as gas ovens, conventional ovens and convection ovens will require different baking times.

Cool the beef jerky slightly and remove the pick from each strip. Blot any remaining fat from the strips with paper towels to prevent the fat from congealing and turning rancid. Store in an airtight container or freeze for longer storage periods.

You may substitute turkey tenderloin for the London broil.

Makes 20 to 30 jerky strips

Helpful Hint

Jerky is great for camping, fishing, or ski trips as it is portable without needing refrigeration, and kids of all ages like it. This in an improvement on the Best Beef Jerky recipe in Cook's Collage, *because hanging the beef strips is a more efficient way to dry them and the London broil is leaner than brisket.*

SWEET-AND-SOUR STUFFED PEPPERS

1 pound ground beef
1 onion, chopped
1 garlic clove, minced
3/4 cup tomato purée
3 tablespoons sherry
2 tablespoons red wine vinegar
2 tablespoons brown sugar
1/4 cup raisins
2 teaspoons salt
1/2 teaspoon cinnamon
1/4 teaspoon ground cloves
1 cup cooked rice
6 large green bell peppers
salt and pepper to taste
1/3 cup chopped fresh parsley
1/3 cup chopped red bell pepper

Cook the ground beef with the onion and garlic in a large skillet until the ground beef is brown and crumbly and the vegetables are tender; drain. Add the tomato purée, sherry, vinegar, brown sugar, raisins, 2 teaspoons salt, cinnamon and cloves and mix well. Cook over medium heat for 20 minutes, stirring occasionally. Remove from the heat and cool for 10 minutes. Stir in the rice.

Remove the tops, seeds and membranes from the green bell peppers. Bring 1 inch of water to a boil in a large saucepan fitted with a steamer rack. Arrange the green bell peppers cut ends down on the steamer rack. Steam, covered, for 10 minutes.

Arrange the green bell peppers cut ends up in a buttered baking dish just large enough to hold them upright. Sprinkle the inside of each bell pepper with salt and pepper to taste.

Spoon the ground beef mixture into the green bell peppers. Sprinkle with the parsley and red bell pepper and cover loosely with foil. Bake at 375 degrees for 20 minutes.

Serves 6

Photograph for this recipe appears on page 120.

TIJUANA TORTE

1 pound ground beef
1 medium onion, chopped
1 (16-ounce) can stewed or diced tomatoes
1 (8-ounce) can tomato sauce
1 (4-ounce) can chopped green chiles
1 envelope taco seasoning mix
6 to 8 flour tortillas
16 ounces shredded Cheddar cheese
1 to 1¹/₂ cups sour cream (optional)

Cook the ground beef with the onion in a skillet until the ground beef is brown and crumbly and the onion is tender; drain. Add the tomatoes, tomato sauce, green chiles and taco seasoning mix and stir to mix well. Simmer for 10 to 15 minutes, stirring occasionally.

Spread ¹/₄ cup of the ground beef mixture in a 9×13-inch baking dish. Layer half the tortillas, half the remaining ground beef mixture and half the cheese in the prepared dish. Spread with the sour cream and layer the remaining tortillas, ground beef mixture and cheese over the top. Bake at 350 degrees for 25 minutes or until the cheese is bubbly.

Serves 6 to 8

WINE SUGGESTION: *Grenache*

VEAL AND ASPARAGUS ROLLS

1 (16-ounce) package lasagna
  noodles
1/4 cup olive oil
3 yellow onions, chopped
4 garlic cloves, minced
2 ribs celery, finely chopped
2 bunches asparagus, cut into 1-inch
  pieces
1 pound ground veal
2 cups ricotta cheese
6 ounces shredded provolone cheese
  or fontina cheese

2 eggs, lightly beaten
2 tablespoons minced fresh oregano
2 tablespoons minced fresh thyme
1 teaspoon salt
1/8 teaspoon pepper
1/4 cup (1/2 stick) butter
1/4 cup flour
3 cups warm milk
6 tablespoons pesto
1/4 cup freshly grated Parmesan
  cheese

Cook the lasagna noodles using the package directions. Drain and plunge into a large bowl of ice water to prevent noodles from sticking together; set aside.

Heat the olive oil in a large sauté pan over medium-high heat until hot. Add the onions, garlic and celery and sauté for 3 to 4 minutes or until tender, stirring constantly. Add the asparagus and cook for 9 to 10 minutes or until tender, stirring frequently. Set aside to cool.

Brown the veal in a skillet, stirring until crumbly; drain. Add the ricotta cheese, provolone cheese, eggs, oregano, thyme, salt and pepper and mix well. Stir in the asparagus mixture.

Drain the lasagna noodles and place flat on waxed paper or foil. Spoon equal amounts of the veal mixture evenly over the surface of each noodle and carefully roll to enclose the filling. Stand the stuffed rolled noodles on end in a deep baking dish.

Melt the butter in a medium saucepan over medium heat. Add the flour and cook over low heat for 1 to 2 minutes or until smooth and bubbly but not brown, stirring constantly. Stir in the warm milk gradually and cook over medium-low heat for 6 to 8 minutes or until thickened, stirring constantly. Spoon over the lasagna rolls. Top with the pesto and sprinkle with the Parmesan cheese.

Bake, covered loosely with foil, at 350 degrees for 45 minutes. Remove the foil and bake for 20 minutes longer or just until the cheese is bubbly and light brown.

Serves 6 to 8

WINE SUGGESTION: *Full-bodied Viognier*

GLADYS SCIVALLY'S VEAL ROSEMARY

8 ounces fresh mushrooms, sliced
1 tablespoon butter
2 pounds veal, cut into cubes
flour for coating
salt and pepper to taste
2 garlic cloves
$^{1}/_{4}$ cup ($^{1}/_{2}$ stick) butter
1 cup white port
$^{3}/_{4}$ cup heavy cream
1 teaspoon rosemary

Sauté the mushrooms in 1 tablespoon butter in a small skillet over medium heat until tender; set aside. Coat the veal in a mixture of flour, salt and pepper.

Cook the garlic in $^{1}/_{4}$ cup butter in a medium skillet until tender, stirring constantly. Discard the garlic. Add the veal to the hot butter in the skillet and sear on all sides over medium-high heat until golden brown, stirring constantly. Stir in the port and reduce the heat to low. Simmer, covered, for 1 hour.

Stir in the cream, rosemary and sautéed mushrooms. Cook, uncovered, for 10 minutes or until the sauce thickens. Serve over wild rice with a fruit salad.

Serves 6

WINE SUGGESTION: *Roussanne*

VEAL SCALOPPINE IN LEMON SAUCE

4 veal cutlets
1/2 cup flour
3/4 teaspoon salt
3/4 teaspoon freshly ground pepper
2 tablespoons butter or margarine
1 tablespoon olive oil
2 tablespoons butter or margarine
1/2 cup dry white wine
3 tablespoons lemon juice
2 tablespoons chopped fresh parsley
2 large garlic cloves, crushed
2 tablespoons capers

Flatten the veal to 1/4-inch thickness between 2 sheets of heavy-duty plastic wrap using a meat mallet or rolling pin. Mix the flour, salt and pepper in a shallow dish and add the veal, coating well.

Heat 2 tablespoons butter with the olive oil in a large skillet over medium-high heat until the butter is melted. Add the veal in batches and cook for 1 minute on each side or until golden brown. Remove to a serving platter and keep warm.

Add 2 tablespoons butter, wine and lemon juice to the skillet and stir to loosen any browned particles from the bottom. Cook until heated through, stirring frequently. Stir in the parsley, garlic and capers. Spoon the sauce over the veal to serve.

You may substitute 4 boneless skinless chicken breasts for the veal and increase the cooking time to 3 minutes on each side.

Serves 4

WINE SUGGESTION: *Pouilly-Fuissé*

ROAST LAMB WITH BALSAMIC VINAIGRETTE

$2^{1}/2$ pounds trimmed boneless lamb shoulder, cut into $1^{1}/2$- to 2-inch pieces
1 cup dry white wine
2 carrots, chopped
2 ribs celery, chopped
1 large onion, sliced
$^{1}/2$ cup olive oil
$^{1}/4$ cup balsamic vinegar
3 sprigs of rosemary, or 1 teaspoon crumbled dried rosemary
$^{1}/2$ teaspoon salt
$^{1}/4$ teaspoon pepper
2 cups beef stock

Combine the lamb with the wine, carrots, celery, onion, olive oil, vinegar, rosemary, salt and pepper in a large bowl and mix well. Marinate, covered, for 18 to 24 hours, stirring occasionally.

Place the lamb and marinade in a roasting pan large enough to hold the lamb in a single layer. Add the beef stock. Roast, covered, at 425 degrees for 2 hours. Remove from the oven and reduce the oven temperature to 375 degrees.

Remove the lamb to a medium bowl with a slotted spoon. Strain the remaining mixture through a fine sieve into a heavy medium saucepan, pressing the solids to extract as much liquid as possible. Discard the solids and skim the fat from the strained sauce. Boil the sauce for 30 minutes or until reduced to $^{3}/4$ cup, stirring occasionally.

Return the lamb and the reduced sauce to the roasting pan, stirring to coat the lamb evenly. Bake, uncovered, at 375 degrees for 35 minutes or until the lamb is tender and the sauce is reduced to a rich glaze, stirring every 10 minutes. Remove to a serving platter and garnish with additional rosemary sprigs.

You may cover the lamb and the sauce and store in the refrigerator for up to 24 hours before the final baking time if desired. Bring to room temperature before finishing.

Serves 6

WINE SUGGESTION: *Northern Rhône Syrah*

Grilled Rosemary Lamb Chops

HELPFUL HINT

Rosemary is the ancient symbol of remembrance and friendship. It has a special affinity for lamb dishes.

3/4 cup balsamic vinegar
6 tablespoons olive oil
3 tablespoons fresh lemon juice
3 tablespoons minced fresh rosemary, or
   1 tablespoon dried rosemary
6 garlic cloves, minced
1 teaspoon pepper
12 (1-inch) lamb loin chops, trimmed
salt and pepper to taste

Combine the vinegar, olive oil, lemon juice, rosemary, garlic and 1 teaspoon pepper in a small bowl and whisk until well mixed. Arrange the lamb chops in a single layer in a 9×13-inch glass dish and pour the vinegar mixture over the top. Marinate, covered with foil, for 4 hours, turning occasionally. Drain the lamb chops, reserving the marinade. Season with salt and pepper to taste.

Grill, covered, for 4 minutes on each side for medium-rare or until done to taste, basting often with the reserved marinade; discard any remaining marinade.

You may soak $1^1/2$ cups mesquite wood chips in cold water for 1 hour and add to the hot coals to grill. Add the lamb chops when the chips begin to smoke.

Serves 4

Wine Suggestion: *Napa Merlot*

HAM LOAF

MUSTARD BASTING SAUCE
1 tablespoon brown sugar
2 teaspoons vinegar
1 teaspoon dry mustard
paprika to taste

HAM LOAF
2 pounds lean ground pork
1 pound ground cured ham
1 cup cracker crumbs
1 cup milk
1 egg, beaten
1 teaspoon salt
pepper to taste

TO PREPARE THE BASTING SAUCE, combine the brown sugar, vinegar, mustard and paprika in a small bowl and mix well. Add enough water to make a thin paste.

TO PREPARE THE LOAF, combine the ground pork, ground ham, cracker crumbs, milk, egg, salt and pepper in a large bowl and mix well. Press evenly into a greased ring mold or greased large loaf pan. Bake at 275 degrees for 2 hours, basting occasionally with the sauce.

Unmold or remove from the pan onto a serving plate. Serve with prepared horseradish sauce.

Serves 8 to 10

WINE SUGGESTION: *Cru Beaujolais*

In 1927, Claude Terwilleger developed Terwilleger Heights, a highly desirable residential area. During platting for his subdivision, he learned he was working above a rich deposit of oil with an estimated minimum production of 500 barrels of oil per day. Although tempted to begin drilling, Terwilleger considered the damage it would cause in Tulsa's future development and instead chose to further develop the subdivision until its completion in 1933. The subdivision still exists today.

CREOLE PORK TENDERLOIN WITH ORANGE AND RED ONION SALSA

ORANGE AND RED ONION SALSA

sections of 1 peeled navel orange
1 red onion, finely chopped
1 teaspoon minced garlic
1 teaspoon minced serrano chiles
2 tablespoons chopped fresh cilantro
1 teaspoon cumin

1 teaspoon Tony Chachere's
   Seasoning
salt and freshly cracked pepper to
   taste
5 tablespoons lime juice

PORK TENDERLOIN

4 green onions, finely chopped
4 garlic cloves, minced
2 serranos, finely chopped
1 teaspoon salt
2 tablespoons Tony Chachere's
   Seasoning

2 teaspoons cider vinegar
1/4 cup vegetable oil
2 (10- to 12-ounce) pork
   tenderloins

TO PREPARE THE SALSA, combine the orange, red onion, garlic, chiles, cilantro, cumin, Tony Chachere's Seasoning, salt, pepper and lime juice in a medium bowl and mix well. Chill, covered, for up to 3 days.

TO PREPARE THE PORK TENDERLOIN, combine the green onions, garlic, chiles, salt, Tony Chachere's Seasoning, vinegar and vegetable oil in a sealable plastic bag. Add the pork and seal the bag, kneading until the ingredients are well mixed and the pork is coated. Marinate for 2 to 4 hours. Drain, discarding the marinade.

Insert a meat thermometer into the thickest portion of the pork. Grill the pork over medium heat to 135 degrees on the meat thermometer or until cooked through. Remove from heat and let stand for 10 minutes before slicing.

To serve, slice the pork into 1/4-inch-thick medallions and top with the salsa.

Serves 6

BEVERAGE SUGGESTION: *Sauvignon Blanc or Beer*

HERB-CRUSTED PORK TENDERLOIN

3 pounds pork tenderloins, trimmed
salt and pepper to taste
2 eggs, beaten
6 cups seasoned bread crumbs
1/4 cup (1/2 stick) butter
2 tablespoons olive oil

Sprinkle the pork with salt and pepper and dip in the beaten eggs. Roll in the bread crumbs, coating completely.

Melt half the butter with half the olive oil in a heavy skillet over medium-high heat. Add half the pork and cook until golden brown on all sides, turning frequently. Remove to a roasting pan and wipe the grease from the skillet with paper towels. Repeat the browning process with the remaining butter, olive oil and pork. Remove the pork to the roasting pan.

Insert a meat thermometer into the thickest portion of the pork. Roast at 375 degrees for 20 minutes or to 155 degrees on the meat thermometer. Remove from the oven and let stand for 5 minutes. Slice and serve with creamy polenta and homemade cranberry sauce. Garnish with fresh rosemary.

Serves 8

WINE SUGGESTION: *White Burgundy*

HELPFUL HINT

Warm Green Olives are a good complement to pork. Combine 8 ounces mixed green olives and 3 sprigs of fresh thyme in the center of a 12×12-inch piece of foil and fold the foil into a 5-inch-square packet, sealing the edges completely. Bake at 450 degrees for 15 minutes or until the olives are warm and juicy.

PORK CAMBAZOLA

HELPFUL HINT

Cambazola is a modern bleu cheese made from cow's milk. It has a smooth, rich texture with a savory and slightly sweet taste.

1 apple, cored, thinly sliced
1 tablespoon butter
1 cup dry vermouth
1 teaspoon crushed red pepper
1 cup heavy cream
1/4 cup crumbled cambazola cheese
salt and black pepper to taste
1 pound pork tenderloin
2 tablespoons olive oil

Sauté the apple in the butter in a medium sauté pan over medium heat until brown. Add the vermouth and reduce until almost no liquid remains. Add the red pepper, cream and cheese and stir to mix well. Simmer over low heat until thickened, stirring frequently. Season the sauce with salt and black pepper and keep warm over very low heat.

Brown the pork in the olive oil in a large skillet over medium-high heat, turning to brown all sides. Remove to a roasting pan. Roast at 350 degrees for 10 to 15 minutes or until cooked through. Remove and let stand for 10 minutes. Slice the pork and serve with the cheese sauce.

Serves 4

WINE SUGGESTION: *Lugana*

Roast Loin of Pork with Pistachio Filling

8 ounces mild Italian sausage, casings removed, crumbled
1/2 cup unsalted pistachio nuts, coarsely chopped
1/4 cup fresh bread crumbs
1 (4-pound) boneless top loin pork roast, tied
2 teaspoons quatre épices
salt and pepper to taste
6 medium Yukon gold potatoes, cut into 1-inch cubes
1 tablespoon olive oil
2/3 cup apple cider

HELPFUL HINT

Quatre épices is French for "four spices." It includes a blend of 2 parts each fresh ground white pepper, nutmeg and ginger to 1 part cinnamon or ground cloves.

Combine the sausage, pistachios and bread crumbs in a small bowl and mix well. Untie the roast and pat the sausage mixture over half of the open roast. Close and retie the roast, and place in a lightly greased large roasting pan. Rub the entire surface of the roast with the quatre épices, salt and pepper. Insert a meat thermometer into the thickest portion of the roast. Roast at 325 degrees for 1 hour.

Toss the potatoes with the olive oil in a large bowl and add to the roasting pan. Roast for 50 to 60 minutes longer or until the potatoes are tender and the meat thermometer registers 160 to 170 degrees, turning the potatoes frequently. Remove the roast and potatoes to a warm serving platter and tent with foil to keep warm.

Place the roasting pan over 2 stove burners and skim and discard any fat from the drippings in the pan. Add the cider and bring to a boil over medium heat, stirring constantly. Stir to deglaze the pan, scraping and stirring any browned particles from the bottom of the pan. Season with salt and pepper. Serve with the sliced roast.

Serves 8

WINE SUGGESTION: *Lightly-oaked Fumé Blanc*

ROAST PORK LOIN

HELPFUL HINT

Gruyère cheese is made from cow's milk and has a nutty flavor. Like other Swiss cheeses, it has holes.

1 (3-pound) pork loin roast, rolled, tied
salt and pepper to taste
1/4 cup (1/2 stick) unsalted butter
2 large Vidalia or Spanish onions, sliced
1 teaspoon salt
1/2 teaspoon pepper
1 cup dry white wine
1 cup shredded Gruyère cheese

Season the roast with salt and pepper to taste and place in a roasting pan; insert a meat thermometer into the thickest portion. Roast at 350 degrees for 1 1/2 hours or to 165 degrees on the meat thermometer. Remove from the oven and let stand for 20 minutes.

Melt the butter in a medium sauté pan over medium heat. Add the onions, 1 teaspoon salt and 1/2 teaspoon pepper. Cook, covered, over medium heat until the onions are tender, stirring frequently.

Stir in the wine and simmer, uncovered, until the liquid is almost evaporated. Remove from the heat. Slice the roast and arrange on an ovenproof serving platter. Spoon the onion mixture evenly over the top and sprinkle with the cheese. Roast at 350 degrees just until the cheese is melted and light brown.

Serves 6 to 8

WINE SUGGESTION: *White Burgundy*

SPICY BLACK BEAN ENCHILADAS

1 medium green bell pepper, chopped
4 medium green onions, thinly sliced
1 (4-ounce) can chopped green chiles
2 (15-ounce) cans black beans, rinsed, drained
1 tablespoon vinegar
2 teaspoons grated lime zest
1/2 teaspoon hot red pepper sauce
1 (14-ounce) can red enchilada sauce
1 (14-ounce) can green enchilada sauce
8 (6-inch) flour tortillas
1 cup shredded nonfat Cheddar cheese

Cook the bell pepper and green onions in a large skillet sprayed with nonstick cooking spray over medium heat until tender, stirring frequently. Add 1/4 cup of the green chiles, beans, vinegar, lime zest and hot red pepper sauce and mix well. Cook until heated through, stirring occasionally. Remove from the heat and set aside.

Combine the red and green enchilada sauces and remaining chiles in a medium bowl and mix well. Dip each tortilla into the enchilada sauce mixture and spoon 1/2 cup of the bean mixture into the center of each dipped tortilla. Roll the tortillas to enclose the filling and arrange in a 9×13-inch baking dish sprayed with nonstick cooking spray.

Sprinkle with the cheese and top with the remaining enchilada sauce mixture. Bake, covered, at 350 degrees for 20 to 25 minutes or until the cheese is melted and bubbly.

Serves 8

WINE SUGGESTION: *Red Zinfandel*

ROASTED CHICKEN WITH MUSTARD VINAIGRETTE

MUSTARD VINAIGRETTE
1/4 cup Dijon mustard
3 tablespoons white wine vinegar
3/4 cup olive oil
2/3 cup chopped shallots
2 tablespoons chopped fresh
   rosemary

2 teaspoons chopped fresh sage
1/4 teaspoon salt
1/2 teaspoon coarsely ground pepper

CHICKEN
1 (6- to 7-pound) roasting chicken
salt and pepper to taste
2 shallots, cut into quarters
2 sprigs of rosemary

2 sprigs of sage
1 tablespoon chopped fresh
   rosemary
1 tablespoon chopped fresh sage

TO PREPARE THE VINAIGRETTE, combine the mustard and vinegar in a medium bowl and mix well. Whisk in the olive oil gradually. Stir in the shallots, rosemary, sage, salt and pepper.

TO PREPARE THE CHICKEN, discard the neck and giblets. Season the cavity with salt and pepper. Place the shallots and sprigs of rosemary and sage inside the cavity. Lift the breast skin, forming a pocket, and spread 2 tablespoons of the mustard vinaigrette between the skin and breast meat. Truss the legs and tuck the wings under the body of the chicken.

Place the chicken in a roasting pan and brush the entire outer surface of the chicken with 2 tablespoons of the Mustard Vinaigrette. Sprinkle with the chopped rosemary and sage and season with salt and pepper.

Roast at 450 degrees for 20 minutes. Reduce the oven temperature to 375 degrees. Roast for 1 hour and 20 minutes longer or until the juices run clear when the thickest part of the thigh is pierced, basting occasionally with the pan juices.

Remove to a platter and garnish with additional sprigs of rosemary and sage. Serve with Potatoes and Green Beans with Bleu Cheese and Walnuts (page 198). The Mustard Vinaigrette yields enough vinaigrette for both dishes.

Serves 4 to 6

WINE SUGGESTION: *Rhône White*

STONEHORSE CAFÉ'S CHICKEN WITH FORTY CLOVES OF GARLIC

1 (2¹/2- to 3-pound) chicken
salt and pepper to taste
flour for coating
3 tablespoons olive oil
¹/2 cup garlic cloves

1 large sweet yellow onion,
  julienned
2 tablespoons Champagne vinegar
1¹/2 cups chicken stock
fresh thyme leaves

Split the chicken into halves and season both sides with salt and pepper. Coat lightly with flour. Heat the olive oil in a large braising pan over high heat. Add the chicken and sear on both sides; do not overbrown the flour coating. Remove the chicken to a platter.

Add the garlic and onion to the remaining hot oil in the pan and cook over low heat until caramelized, stirring occasionally. Add the vinegar and stock and stir to deglaze the pan, scraping any browned particles from the bottom of the pan. Add the thyme and the chicken halves and braise, tightly covered, in the oven at 325 degrees for 1¹/2 hours or until cooked through. Serve with sautéed spinach and roasted new potatoes.

Serves 4

BASIL CREAM CHICKEN

¹/2 cup minced onion
1 tablespoon butter or olive oil
6 boneless skinless chicken breasts
1 (28-ounce) can diced plum
  tomatoes, drained
³/4 cup heavy cream

1 (14-ounce) can artichoke hearts,
  drained (optional)
¹/2 cup fresh basil leaves, chopped
salt and black pepper to taste
1 teaspoon red pepper flakes

Sauté the onion in the butter in a large skillet over medium heat until translucent, stirring constantly. Add the chicken and cook for 5 minutes on each side or until no longer pink. Remove the chicken to a greased 9×13-inch baking dish.

Add the tomatoes, cream and artichokes to the onion in the skillet. Bring to a boil over medium-high heat, stirring constantly. Add the basil, salt, black pepper and red pepper flakes and mix well. Pour over the chicken in the prepared dish. Bake at 425 degrees for 30 to 40 minutes or until cooked through. Serve over hot cooked pasta if desired.

Serves 6

WINE SUGGESTION: *Rich Chardonnay*

CHICKEN MARIA

2 cups chicken stock
$1/4$ teaspoon minced garlic
1 teaspoon lemon juice
$1/3$ cup sherry
$1/2$ cup (1 stick) butter
$1/4$ cup flour
$1^1/2$ cups shredded provolone cheese
$1/2$ teaspoon cracked pepper
2 cups sliced fresh mushrooms
1 cup lump crab meat
6 to 8 boneless skinless chicken breasts
salt and pepper to taste
flour for coating
2 tablespoons butter
18 to 24 fresh asparagus spears

Combine the chicken stock, garlic, lemon juice and sherry in a medium saucepan and mix well. Bring the mixture to a boil over high heat, stirring constantly. Melt $1/2$ cup butter in a small skillet over medium heat and add $1/4$ cup flour; cook until bubbly and golden brown, stirring constantly. Add to the boiling chicken stock mixture and cook until thickened, stirring constantly.

Reduce the heat to low and add the cheese, $1/2$ teaspoon cracked pepper, mushrooms and crab meat. Cook until the cheese melts, stirring to mix well.

Season the chicken with salt and pepper to taste and coat with flour. Brown the chicken in 2 tablespoons butter in a medium skillet over medium heat, turning to brown both sides. Reduce the heat and cook until chicken is cooked through; keep warm.

Steam the asparagus spears in a steamer until tender-crisp. Place 1 chicken breast on each serving plate and top with 3 asparagus spears. Top with the mushroom sauce.

Serves 6 to 8

WINE SUGGESTION: *Châteauneuf-du-Pape Blanc*

GOAT CHEESE–STUFFED CHICKEN WITH MUSHROOM SAUCE

MUSHROOM SAUCE
1/2 cup (1 stick) butter
1 pound mushrooms, sliced
1/2 cup dry white wine

1 1/3 cups low-sodium chicken broth
1/4 cup (1/2 stick) butter, cut into
    quarters

CHICKEN
4 boneless skinless chicken breasts
1/2 cup crumbled goat cheese
2 green onions, thinly sliced
1 tablespoon thinly sliced basil
1/4 cup oil-pack sun-dried tomatoes,
    drained, chopped

salt and freshly ground pepper to
    taste
1 egg, beaten
1/2 cup dry bread crumbs
2 tablespoons butter, melted

TO PREPARE THE SAUCE, melt 1/2 cup butter in a Dutch oven or heavy large skillet over medium heat. Add the mushrooms and sauté until tender. Add the wine and bring to a boil, stirring constantly. Boil for 3 minutes, stirring constantly. Add the broth and cook until reduced by 1/2. Remove from the heat and stir in 1/4 cup butter 1 tablespoon at a time.

TO PREPARE THE CHICKEN, pound the chicken 1/4 inch thick between sheets of waxed paper with a meat mallet. Pat the chicken dry. Combine the goat cheese, green onions, basil and sun-dried tomatoes in a small bowl and mix well. Season with salt and pepper.

Spread the mixture evenly over half of each chicken breast. Tuck the tapered ends under and roll from the long side to enclose the filling; tie the ends with kitchen twine.

Dip the chicken into the beaten egg in a shallow dish, allowing any excess to drip back into the dish. Coat with the bread crumbs, shaking to remove any excess. Arrange in an 8-inch square baking dish and drizzle with the melted butter. Bake at 350 degrees for 30 to 35 minutes or until cooked through.

To serve, remove the kitchen twine and serve the chicken over a bed of cooked wild rice. Serve with the mushroom sauce.

Serves 4

WINE SUGGESTION: *Pouilly-Fumé*

Lemon Chicken Kabobs

Kabobs

1/3 cup fresh lemon juice
1 tablespoon grated lemon zest
1/4 cup vegetable oil
1 tablespoon sugar
1 tablespoon vinegar
2 teaspoons salt
1/4 teaspoon cayenne pepper

1 garlic clove, minced
4 whole boneless chicken breasts,
   cut into large pieces or strips
3 medium zucchini, cut into 1-inch
   pieces
8 ounces whole mushrooms

Lemon Butter

1/4 cup (1/2 stick) butter, melted
1 tablespoon lemon juice
1 tablespoon chopped parsley

1/2 teaspoon salt
cayenne pepper to taste

To prepare the kabobs, combine the lemon juice, lemon zest, vegetable oil, sugar, vinegar, salt, cayenne pepper and garlic in a small bowl and whisk to mix well. Combine with the chicken, zucchini and mushrooms in a sealable plastic bag. Seal the bag and marinate in the refrigerator for 3 hours or longer, turning occasionally.

Drain the chicken and vegetables, reserving the marinade. Thread the chicken and vegetables onto skewers. Grill over medium coals for 20 to 30 minutes or until brown and cooked through, turning and basting occasionally with the reserved marinade. Discard any remaining marinade.

To prepare the lemon butter, combine the butter, lemon juice, parsley, salt and cayenne pepper in a small bowl and whisk to mix well. Serve with the kabobs and garnish with lemon slices and sprigs of parsley.

Serves 4

Wine Suggestion: *Light White from Macon*

CHICKEN CREPES FLORENTINE

SWISS CHEESE SAUCE WITH MUSHROOMS

1/2 cup (1 stick) butter
1/2 cup flour
1 cup chicken stock
2 cups milk
1 teaspoon salt

white pepper to taste
1/2 teaspoon dry mustard
8 ounces mushrooms, sliced
2 tablespoons butter
1 cup shredded Swiss cheese

CREPES

1 medium onion, chopped
1/4 cup (1/2 stick) butter
2 tablespoons vegetable oil
1/2 teaspoon basil
dried mint, nutmeg and white
   pepper to taste
1 teaspoon salt

3 or 4 whole boneless chicken
   breasts, cooked, chopped
1 (10-ounce) package frozen
   chopped spinach, cooked, drained
1 cup reserved sauce
12 crepes
1/2 cup shredded Swiss cheese

TO PREPARE THE SAUCE, melt 1/2 cup butter in a medium saucepan over low heat. Stir in the flour and cook for 2 minutes, stirring constantly. Heat the stock and milk in a medium saucepan over medium heat. Whisk into the flour mixture. Add the salt, white pepper and dry mustard and cook over medium heat until smooth and thickened, stirring constantly. Reserve 1 cup of the sauce. Sauté the mushrooms in 2 tablespoons butter in a skillet over medium-high heat for 5 minutes, stirring constantly. Add the mushrooms and cheese to the remaining sauce and mix well.

TO PREPARE THE CREPES, sauté the onion in the butter and vegetable oil in a large sauté pan over medium heat until tender. Add the basil, mint, nutmeg, white pepper, salt, chicken, spinach and the reserved 1 cup sauce; mix well.

To assemble, spoon the filling evenly onto the crepes and roll to enclose the filling. Arrange the crepes seam side down in a buttered baking dish. Spread the remaining Swiss cheese sauce evenly over the top and sprinkle with the cheese.

Bake at 350 degrees for 30 to 45 minutes or until the crepes are heated through and the cheese is light brown.

You may prepare this dish in advance, wrap and freeze until needed. Thaw completely before baking as directed.

Serves 6

WINE SUGGESTION: *Viognier*

Enchiladas Verdes

Hot Salsa
2 large tomatoes
1 medium onion, finely chopped
6 to 8 jalapeño chiles, seeded,
   chopped

1/2 teaspoon salt
1 garlic clove, chopped
1 teaspoon vegetable oil

Spinach Sauce
1 (10-ounce) package frozen
   chopped spinach, thawed
3 to 4 green onions, chopped
2 jalapeño chiles, seeded
1 (10-ounce) can cream of chicken
   soup

salt and freshly ground pepper
   to taste
2 cups sour cream or low-fat
   sour cream

Enchiladas
4 cups shredded Monterey Jack
   cheese
1 onion, finely chopped
shredded cooked chicken (optional)

20 (6-inch) corn tortillas
3 cups shredded Monterey Jack
   cheese

To prepare the salsa, cook the unpeeled tomatoes in 1 inch of boiling water in a medium saucepan for 5 minutes. Drain, reserving the cooking liquid. Peel and coarsely chop the tomatoes. Combine the tomatoes, onion, jalapeños, salt, garlic, vegetable oil and 1/2 cup of the reserved cooking liquid in a medium saucepan and cook over medium heat for 5 minutes, stirring frequently. Cool to room temperature.

To prepare the sauce, drain the spinach, pressing out the excess moisture. Combine the spinach, green onions, jalapeños, soup, salt and pepper in a blender and blend until well mixed. Add the sour cream and blend until smooth.

To prepare the enchiladas, combine 4 cups cheese, onion and chicken in a bowl and mix well. Steam the tortillas in a steamer to soften. Spoon the chicken mixture down the centers of the tortillas and roll the tortillas to enclose the filling. Arrange seam side down in a 9×13-inch baking dish sprayed with nonstick cooking spray.

Pour the spinach sauce evenly over the enchiladas and top with 3 cups cheese. Bake at 350 degrees for 30 to 45 minutes or until bubbly. Serve with the salsa.

Serves 10

Beverage Suggestion: *Dry Riesling or Beer*

INDIAN SUMMER CHICKEN AND SQUASH

1 (10-ounce) package frozen chopped spinach, thawed
3 medium yellow squash, thinly sliced
1 large red bell pepper, cut into 1/2-inch pieces
1 yellow onion, thinly sliced
2 tablespoons peanut oil
3 cups shredded cooked chicken or turkey
12 (6-inch) corn tortillas, cut into 1-inch pieces
1 (10-ounce) can cream of celery soup
1 (8-ounce) jar picante sauce
1 (4-ounce) can chopped green chiles
1 envelope fajita seasoning
2 cups shredded sharp Cheddar cheese

Drain the spinach, pressing out the excess moisture. Sauté the squash, bell pepper and onion in the peanut oil in a large skillet over medium-high heat for 6 minutes or until tender, stirring constantly. Remove from the heat and stir in the spinach, chicken, tortillas, soup, picante sauce, undrained green chiles, fajita seasoning and 1 1/2 cups of the cheese.

Spoon into a lightly greased 9×13-inch baking dish. Bake at 350 degrees for 30 minutes. Sprinkle with the remaining 1/2 cup cheese and bake for 5 minutes longer.

Serves 6 to 8

WINE SUGGESTION: *Alsace Pinot Blanc*

OIL CAPITAL CHICKEN FLORENTINE

2 (10-ounce) packages frozen
   chopped spinach, cooked, drained
16 ounces cream cheese, softened
3 cups milk
2 cups shredded Monterey Jack
   cheese
1 cup grated Parmesan cheese

1/2 teaspoon salt
1/4 teaspoon paprika
1/2 teaspoon garlic powder
4 cups shredded cooked
   chicken breasts
2 cups cooked rotini
bread crumbs

Spread the spinach in a greased 9×13-inch baking dish. Beat the cream cheese in a medium bowl until smooth and fluffy. Add the milk gradually, beating constantly until smooth and creamy. Add the cheeses, salt, paprika and garlic powder and mix well.

Pour half the cheese mixture over the spinach and layer evenly with the chicken and pasta. Spread the remaining cheese mixture over the top and sprinkle with the bread crumbs. Bake at 350 degrees for 30 minutes. Serve with crusty bread and a fruit salad.

Serves 8

WINE SUGGESTION: *Viognier*

STUFFED CORNISH HENS ORIENTAL

1 cup small seasoned croutons
1/4 cup (1/2 stick) butter, melted
1/4 cup golden raisins or dried
   cranberries, or a mixture
1/4 cup drained mandarin oranges,
   chopped
1/4 apple, thinly sliced

1/4 cup soy sauce
6 (16- to 24-ounce) Cornish game
   hens
1 garlic clove, crushed
1 to 2 cups Kikkoman Teriyaki
   Baste and Glaze

Combine the croutons, butter, raisins, oranges, apple and soy sauce in a small bowl and mix well. Spoon into the game hen cavities. Combine the garlic and Baste and Glaze and whisk to mix well. Brush over the game hens and arrange breast side up in a baking dish. Roast at 350 degrees for 1 to 1 1/2 hours or until golden brown and the skins are slightly crisp, basting with the remaining basting mixture every 20 minutes. Serve over hot cooked wild rice.

Serves 6

WINE SUGGESTION: *Pinot Gris*

GRILLED SALMON WITH ORANGE GLAZE

1/2 cup orange marmalade
2 garlic cloves, crushed
2 teaspoons sesame oil
2 teaspoons soy sauce
3 tablespoons white rice vinegar
4 (6- to 8-ounce) skinless salmon fillets
6 scallions, thinly sliced
1/4 cup sesame seeds, toasted

Combine the orange marmalade, garlic, sesame oil, soy sauce and vinegar in a small bowl and whisk to mix well. Brush over both sides of the salmon.

Grill over medium coals for 5 minutes on each side or until the fish flakes easily. Top with the scallions and toasted sesame seeds to serve.

Serves 4

WINE SUGGESTION: *Monterey Pinot Noir*

During the early oil boom days, people flocked to Tulsa upon hearing exaggerated stories of oil discoveries. By 1903, there was a housing shortage and "tent cities" were common around oil sites.

GRILLED YELLOWFIN TUNA WITH AVOCADO BUTTER

HELPFUL HINT

Yellowfin tuna, a large member of the mackerel family, is found in Hawaii and other warm waters. In Hawaii it is called ahi.

AVOCADO BUTTER
1/2 cup (1 stick) butter, softened
1 large avocado, coarsely chopped
1/2 cup fresh cilantro leaves
juice of 1 lime
1/8 teaspoon salt
1/8 teaspoon white pepper

TUNA
2 yellowfin tuna steaks
1 tablespoon vegetable oil
1/8 teaspoon salt
1/8 teaspoon white pepper

TO PREPARE THE AVOCADO BUTTER, combine the butter, avocado, cilantro and lime juice in a food processor and process until smooth. Season with the salt and pepper. Spoon the avocado mixture onto waxed paper and shape into a log. Wrap in waxed paper and chill until firm.

TO PREPARE THE TUNA, brush the steaks with the vegetable oil and season with the salt and pepper. Grill or broil the tuna steaks for 3 to 4 minutes on each side or until the steaks flake easily.

Cut the chilled avocado butter into 1/2-inch-thick slices. Top the steaks with the avocado butter to serve.

Serves 2   *Photograph for this recipe appears on page 120.*

WINE SUGGESTION: *White Rhône*

CURRIED SHRIMP WITH RICE

6 ounces dried or flaked coconut
2 cups hot water
1/2 onion, finely chopped
1 garlic clove, minced
1 cinnamon stick
2 cloves
1 teaspoon cumin seeds
2 cardamom pods, or to taste
1 bay leaf
4 1/2 teaspoons canola oil
1 (15-ounce) can diced tomatoes
turmeric to taste
1 teaspoon ginger
1 teaspoon curry powder
1/2 teaspoon salt
cayenne pepper to taste
8 ounces fresh medium shrimp, peeled
hot cooked rice

Soak the coconut in the hot water in a small bowl for 30 minutes to make coconut milk. Drain, reserving the coconut milk and coconut.

Sauté the onion, garlic, cinnamon stick, cloves, cumin, cardamom and bay leaf in the canola oil in a medium sauté pan over medium heat until the onion is tender, stirring constantly. Add the tomatoes, turmeric, ginger, curry powder, salt and cayenne pepper and cook for 2 to 3 minutes, stirring frequently.

Add the shrimp and 1 cup of the coconut milk and bring to a boil, stirring constantly. Reduce the heat and simmer for 30 minutes, stirring occasionally. Add 2 tablespoons of the soaked coconut and stir until the shrimp mixture thickens. Serve over hot cooked rice with a green salad or fried cauliflower and mango smoothies or vanilla frozen yogurt with fresh or canned mango slices for dessert.

Basmati rice is recommended for use in this dish. You may substitute chicken, pork or tofu for the shrimp in this recipe.

Serves 2

WINE SUGGESTION: *Brouilly*

SHRIMP CREOLE

1 cup chopped green bell pepper
2 cups chopped onions
1 cup chopped celery
2 teaspoons minced garlic
$1/2$ cup vegetable oil
2 cups canned whole tomatoes
3 pounds fresh shrimp, peeled, deveined
1 tablespoon paprika
$1/4$ teaspoon cayenne pepper
1 teaspoon salt
$1/4$ teaspoon sugar
3 cups water
1 bay leaf
Tony Chachere's Seasoning (optional)

Sauté the bell pepper, onions, celery and garlic in the vegetable oil in a large sauté pan over medium-high heat until the vegetables are tender, stirring constantly. Add the tomatoes and shrimp and cook over low heat for 2 to 3 minutes. Stir in the paprika, cayenne pepper, salt, sugar, water and bay leaf.

Simmer for 15 minutes, stirring occasionally. Add the seasoning and stir until thickened; discard the bay leaf. Serve over hot cooked rice with a salad.

Serves 6

Shrimp Newburg

Swiss Cheese Sauce
1 cup 1% milk
2 tablespoons flour
1/2 cup shredded Swiss cheese

Shrimp Newburg
1/2 cup chopped onion
2 garlic cloves, minced
1 tablespoon butter or margarine
1 1/4 pounds fresh medium shrimp, peeled, deveined
1/2 cup dry vermouth
8 ounces lump crab meat, shell pieces removed
1 tablespoon chopped fresh chives
1 tablespoon chopped fresh tarragon, or 1 teaspoon dried tarragon
1 tablespoon sherry
1/2 teaspoon salt
1/4 teaspoon ground red pepper
2 1/2 cups hot cooked long grain rice

To prepare the sauce, whisk the milk into the flour in a heavy medium saucepan and cook over medium heat for 8 minutes, stirring constantly. Remove from the heat and add the cheese, stirring until melted.

To prepare the shrimp, sauté the onion and garlic in the butter in a large skillet over medium-high heat for 5 minutes, stirring constantly. Add the shrimp and vermouth and cook for 2 minutes, stirring occasionally.

Add the Swiss cheese sauce, crab meat, chives, tarragon, sherry, salt and red pepper and mix well. Cook for 3 minutes, stirring constantly. Serve over the rice and garnish with additional chives.

For entertaining, spoon into ramekins and broil until light brown; serve with rice.

Serves 5

Wine Suggestion: *Full-bodied Chardonnay*

PASTAS
GRAINS

STRAW AND HAY PASTA

1/4 cup chopped shallots
1/4 cup (1/2 stick) butter
12 ounces fresh mushrooms, sliced
1 teaspoon salt
freshly ground pepper to taste
6 ounces boiled ham or 4 ounces prosciutto, julienned
1/2 cup fresh peas or thawed frozen peas
1 cup heavy cream
salt to taste
1/4 cup (1/2 stick) butter
12 ounces uncooked egg fettuccini
12 ounces uncooked spinach fettuccini
1 cup freshly grated Parmesan cheese

Sauté the shallots in 1/4 cup butter in a large skillet over medium heat until light golden brown, stirring constantly. Increase the heat and add the mushrooms. Cook until the liquid evaporates, stirring constantly. Reduce the heat and add 1 teaspoon salt. Season with pepper.

Increase the heat to high and cook for 3 minutes, stirring frequently. Reduce the heat and stir in the ham and peas. Cook for 1 minute. Add half the cream and cook just until the mixture thickens slightly, stirring constantly. Add salt and pepper to taste and remove from the heat.

Heat the remaining 1/2 cup cream and 1/4 cup butter in a large pan over low heat, stirring until the butter is melted. Remove from the heat.

Cook the pastas separately using the package directions; drain. Add the pastas to the butter and cream mixture. Cook over low heat until heated through, stirring to coat well. Add half the mushroom mixture and mix gently.

Stir in 1/2 cup cheese and heat to serving temperature. Remove to a serving bowl and top with the remaining mushroom mixture. Serve with the remaining cheese. Serve with a tossed green salad and bread.

Serves 8 to 10

WINE SUGGESTION: *Pinot Blanc or White Rhône*

PENNE WITH SPICY SAUSAGE AND PAPRIKA SAUCE

2 tablespoons minced garlic
1 tablespoon minced shallot
1 tablespoon olive oil
16 ounces hot Italian sausage, casings removed
2 tablespoons sweet paprika
1/4 teaspoon cayenne pepper
1 cup chicken broth
1 1/4 cups heavy cream
8 ounces uncooked penne
1/3 cup finely chopped scallions
1/4 cup freshly grated Parmesan cheese
1/4 cup chopped tomato
2 tablespoons chopped fresh basil or 2 teaspoons crumbled dried basil
2 tablespoons chopped fresh oregano or 2 teaspoons crumbled dried oregano
salt and pepper to taste

Sauté the garlic and shallot in the olive oil in a large skillet over medium heat until the garlic is light golden brown, stirring constantly. Add the sausage, paprika and cayenne pepper. Cook until the sausage is crumbly and cooked through, stirring frequently; drain.

Stir in the chicken broth and simmer until the liquid is reduced by 1/2. Stir in the cream and simmer until the liquid is reduced by 1/2.

Cook the pasta using the package directions; drain. Add the pasta, scallions, cheese, tomato, basil and oregano to the sausage mixture and mix well. Season with salt and pepper.

Serves 2

WINE SUGGESTION: *Barbaresco*

BAKED ZITI

8 ounces ground or link sweet or hot Italian sausage, casings removed (optional)
2 tablespoons vegetable oil
1/4 cup (1/2 stick) butter
1/4 cup flour
1 teaspoon salt
1/2 teaspoon ground pepper
2 cups milk
1/2 cup grated Parmesan cheese
8 ounces ziti, cooked, drained
16 ounces cream-style cottage cheese
1 egg
1 tablespoon chopped fresh parsley
1/2 teaspoon salt
1/8 teaspoon ground pepper
4 ounces mozzarella cheese, shredded
paprika to taste

Cook the sausage in the vegetable oil in a small skillet over medium heat for 10 minutes or until light brown, stirring constantly; drain.

Melt the butter in a large saucepan over medium heat. Remove from heat and stir in the flour, 1 teaspoon salt and 1/2 teaspoon pepper. Return the saucepan to the heat and add the milk gradually, stirring constantly. Bring the mixture to a boil and cook until thickened, stirring constantly. Reduce the heat and simmer for 1 minute longer. Remove from the heat and stir in half the Parmesan cheese. Add the pasta and mix well.

Combine the remaining Parmesan cheese, cottage cheese, egg, parsley, 1/2 teaspoon salt and 1/8 teaspoon pepper in a medium bowl and mix well.

Spoon half the pasta mixture into a 2 1/2-quart baking dish. Layer the cottage cheese mixture and the remaining pasta mixture evenly over the top. Sprinkle with the sausage, mozzarella cheese and paprika. Bake, uncovered, at 350 degrees for 30 to 35 minutes or until bubbly.

Serves 6

WINE SUGGESTION: *Sicilian Table Red*

CANNELLONI

HOMEMADE PASTA

3 egg yolks
1 egg
3 tablespoons cold water

4 teaspoons salt
2 cups sifted flour
6 quarts water

BÉCHAMEL SAUCE

1/4 cup (1/2 stick) butter
1/4 cup flour
1 cup half-and-half or Milnot
1 cup chicken stock

1/4 teaspoon nutmeg
1 teaspoon salt
1/3 teaspoon white pepper
2 egg yolks

CANNELLONI

4 ounces fresh mushrooms
2 cups chopped cooked chicken
1/2 cup drained cooked spinach
1/3 cup grated Parmesan cheese
1/4 teaspoon pepper
5 fresh oregano leaves, chopped

1 egg
1 egg yolk
1/2 cup pine nuts
2 cups prepared tomato sauce
1/4 cup grated cheese
butter

TO PREPARE THE PASTA, beat the egg yolks and egg in a mixing bowl. Beat in the cold water and 1 teaspoon salt. Stir in the flour to make a dough and knead by hand on a floured surface until smooth. Roll paper thin on a floured surface. Cut into 3×4-inch rectangles and let stand for 1 hour to dry. Bring 6 quarts water to a boil in a large stockpot and add the remaining salt. Drop the dough rectangles into the boiling water 6 at a time and stir gently to separate. Cook each batch for 5 minutes; drain.

TO PREPARE THE BÉCHAMEL SAUCE, melt the butter in a heavy saucepan over medium heat. Add the flour and cook for 1 minute, stirring constantly. Add the half-and-half and stock and cook until the mixture begins to thicken, stirring constantly. Add the nutmeg, salt and pepper and mix well. Remove from the heat and stir in the egg yolks; keep warm.

TO PREPARE THE CANNELLONI, sauté the mushrooms in a nonstick skillet until tender. Combine with the chicken and spinach in a food processor and pulse once or twice or until coarsely ground. Combine with 1/3 cup cheese, pepper, oregano, egg, egg yolk and pine nuts in a large bowl and mix well with a wooden spoon.

To assemble, place 1 tablespoon or more of the chicken mixture on the lower third of each pasta rectangle and roll to enclose the filling. Pour half the tomato sauce into a 9×13-inch baking dish. Arrange the filled cannelloni side by side in a single layer in the dish. Top with the béchamel sauce and the remaining tomato sauce. Sprinkle with 1/4 cup cheese and dot with butter. Bake, uncovered, at 375 degrees for 20 minutes or until bubbly.

Serves 6

Chicken Lasagna

1/2 cup (1 stick) butter
2 garlic cloves, crushed
1/2 cup flour
1 teaspoon salt
2 cups milk
2 cups water
2 teaspoons instant chicken bouillon granules
2 cups shredded mozzarella cheese
1/2 cup grated Parmesan cheese
1/2 cup chopped onion
1 teaspoon basil
1/2 teaspoon oregano
1/4 teaspoon pepper
12 to 15 uncooked lasagna noodles
2 cups cottage cheese, puréed
2 cups chopped cooked chicken
2 (10-ounce) packages frozen chopped spinach, thawed, squeezed dry
1/2 cup grated Parmesan cheese

Melt the butter in a 2-quart saucepan over low heat. Add the garlic, flour and salt and cook until bubbly, stirring constantly. Remove from the heat and stir in the milk, water and bouillon granules. Return to the heat and bring the mixture to a boil, stirring constantly. Boil for 1 minute or until thickened, stirring constantly.

Reduce the heat and stir in the mozzarella cheese, 1/2 cup Parmesan cheese, onion, basil, oregano and pepper. Cook over low heat until the cheeses are melted, stirring constantly. Remove from the heat.

Spread 1 1/2 cups of the cheese mixture over the bottom of a 9×13-inch baking pan and top with 3 or 4 lasagna noodles. Layer 1 cup of the cottage cheese, 1 1/2 cups of the cheese mixture, 3 or 4 lasagna noodles and the remaining 1 cup cottage cheese over the top. Arrange the chicken and spinach evenly over the cottage cheese and top with the remaining lasagna noodles. Spread with the remaining cheese mixture and sprinkle with 1/2 cup Parmesan cheese.

Bake, uncovered, at 350 degrees for 35 to 40 minutes or until cheeses are bubbling. Let stand for 15 minutes before serving.

Serves 6 to 8

WINE SUGGESTION: *St. Veran*

PASTA WITH CHICKEN AND SPICY PESTO

3 green onions, chopped
1/2 cup chopped cilantro
1/3 cup pecans, toasted
1 tablespoon minced garlic
2 teaspoons chopped seeded jalapeño chiles (optional)
1/4 teaspoon crushed red pepper
1/4 cup olive oil
1 (10-ounce) can (about) chicken broth (optional)
12 ounces uncooked bow tie pasta
1 pound boneless skinless chicken breasts, cooked, chopped
1/2 cup commercial pesto, or Spinach Pesto (page 170)

Sauté the green onions, cilantro, pecans, garlic, jalapeños and crushed red pepper in the olive oil in a skillet over medium heat for 5 minutes, stirring constantly. Stir in enough chicken broth to thin the mixture if needed for the desired consistency.

Cook the pasta using the package directions. Drain the pasta and toss with the sautéed mixture and chicken in a serving bowl. Add the pesto and toss to coat.

Serves 6

Oilman Josh Cosden built Tulsa's first skyscraper, the sixteen-story Cosden or Mid-Continent Building, in 1918. His million-dollar building symbolized Tulsa's spirit of flamboyant growth during the oil boom. The lavish building was built in the art-deco style for which Tulsa is now known.

PAD THAI

HELPFUL HINT

Banh pho or rice stick noodles are thin, flat, translucent rice noodles that are sold in a variety of sizes. The noodles should be soaked for 30 minutes in cold water and boiled for 4 to 7 minutes before being added to any dish. They are most commonly used in pad thai, stir-fried dishes, and soups. Many assortments of these noodles can be purchased fresh or dried in Asian markets and some dried varieties can be found in most supermarkets.

ASIAN SAUCE

1/4 cup chicken broth
3 tablespoons fish sauce
2 tablespoons ketchup
2 tablespoons sugar

1/2 teaspoon crushed red
   pepper
2 tablespoons rice wine
   vinegar

PORK AND SHRIMP STIR-FRY

6 ounces dried (1/4-inch-wide)
   flat rice noodles (banh pho)
3 tablespoons vegetable oil
1 tablespoon minced garlic
4 ounces lean ground pork
4 ounces fresh medium
   shrimp, peeled, deveined,
   cut into halves lengthwise

1 egg, lightly beaten
2 limes, cut into wedges
1 cup bean sprouts
1 green onion, thinly sliced
2 teaspoons coarsely chopped
   dry-roasted peanuts
2 tablespoons chopped
   cilantro

TO PREPARE THE SAUCE, combine the chicken broth, fish sauce, ketchup, sugar, crushed red pepper and vinegar in a small bowl and mix well.

TO PREPARE THE STIR-FRY, soak the noodles in cold water to cover in a bowl for 30 minutes or until soft; drain. Cook in water to cover in a saucepan for 4 to 7 minutes or until nearly tender; drain.

Heat the vegetable oil in a wok or wide sauté pan over high heat. Add the garlic and stir-fry for 10 seconds or until fragrant. Add the pork and stir-fry for 2 minutes. Add the shrimp and stir-fry for 1 minute or just until barely pink.

Stir in the sauce and cook for 1 minute, stirring constantly. Add the noodles, tossing to combine. Stir in the egg and cook for 1 minute or until the egg is cooked, tossing constantly.

To serve, arrange the noodle mixture on a serving platter and surround with the lime wedges and bean sprouts. Sprinkle the green onion, peanuts and cilantro evenly over the top and serve.

If banh pho is unavailable, you may substitute fresh Chinese-style egg noodles and cook using the package directions just until tender.

Serves 4

WINE SUGGESTION: *Alsatian Riesling*

PASTA JAMBALAYA

CREOLE SEASONING
$2^1/2$ teaspoons paprika
2 tablespoons salt
2 tablespoons garlic powder
1 tablespoon each black pepper, onion powder, cayenne pepper,
    dried oregano and dried thyme

JAMBALAYA
$1/2$ cup julienned cooked chicken breast
1 tablespoon olive oil
2 ounces andouille or chorizo sausage, casings removed, crumbled
8 ounces fresh medium shrimp, peeled, deveined
$1/4$ cup chopped scallions
1 tablespoon minced garlic
$1^1/2$ cups heavy cream
$1/4$ teaspoon each Worcestershire sauce and Tabasco sauce
salt to taste
$1/2$ cup grated Parmesan cheese
8 ounces fettuccini, cooked, drained

TO PREPARE THE SEASONING, combine the paprika, salt, garlic
powder, black pepper, onion powder, cayenne pepper, oregano and
thyme in a small bowl and mix well.

TO PREPARE THE JAMBALAYA, toss the chicken with 1 teaspoon of
the Creole seasoning in a small bowl. Heat the olive oil in a large
skillet over high heat. Add the chicken and sauté for 1 minute.
Add the sausage and cook for 1 minute, stirring constantly. Add
the shrimp and $1^1/2$ teaspoons of the Creole seasoning and sauté
for 1 minute.

Stir in the scallions, garlic and cream and cook for 2 minutes. Stir
in the Worcestershire sauce, Tabasco sauce, salt and half the cheese
and simmer for 3 minutes, stirring occasionally.

To serve, combine the pasta with the chicken mixture and toss
until well mixed. Serve with the remaining cheese.

Serves 4

WINE SUGGESTION: *Dry Gewürztraminer*

HELPFUL HINT

*The Creole
seasoning mixture
in the Pasta
Jambalaya recipe
makes about
$1/2$ cup seasoning,
which can be used
for other dishes.
Store remaining
seasoning in an
airtight container.*

MEDITERRANEAN SHRIMP AND PASTA

5 green onions, sliced
3 garlic cloves, minced
2 tablespoons olive oil
2 (6-ounce) jars marinated artichoke hearts
6 Roma tomatoes, chopped
8 ounces sliced mushrooms
1/4 cup dry white wine
2 teaspoons Italian seasoning
salt and pepper to taste
grated Parmesan cheese to taste
1 pound fresh medium shrimp, peeled, deveined
8 ounces fresh fettuccini, cooked, drained

Sauté the green onions and garlic in the olive oil in a large skillet over medium heat until tender, stirring constantly. Add the undrained artichokes, tomatoes, mushrooms, wine, Italian seasoning, salt, pepper and cheese and mix well. Simmer for 20 minutes, stirring occasionally.

Add the shrimp and cook for 5 minutes longer. Place the pasta on a serving platter and top with the shrimp and artichoke sauce. Garnish with additional grated Parmesan cheese.

This dish tastes even better the next day.

Serves 4

WINE SUGGESTION: *White Côtes du Rhône*

SHRIMP LINGUINI WITH SPRING SAUCE

1 cup chopped onion
1 (14-ounce) can artichoke hearts
1 cup chopped carrots
3 tablespoons olive oil
1 (15-ounce) can diced tomatoes
1 1/2 teaspoons basil
1/2 teaspoon salt
1 garlic clove, chopped or pressed
1/2 teaspoon chicken base
1/2 teaspoon sugar
24 fresh large shrimp, cooked, peeled
6 ounces spinach linguini, cooked, drained
grated Parmesan cheese

Cook the onion, artichokes and carrots in the olive oil in a skillet over medium heat for 5 minutes, stirring frequently. Stir in the undrained tomatoes, basil, salt, garlic, chicken base and sugar and simmer, covered, for 10 to 15 minutes.

Serve the shrimp and the artichoke sauce over the linguini in a serving dish and top with Parmesan cheese.

Serves 6

WINE SUGGESTION: *Gavi di Gavi*

SAUTÉED SHRIMP PASTA WITH PESTO

HELPFUL HINT

The pesto in this recipe can be prepared and stored in the refrigerator for 2 days or in the freezer for up to 1 month. It is also delicious as a dip with toast points.

SPINACH PESTO
1 cup packed fresh basil leaves
1/2 cup torn fresh spinach leaves (about 2 ounces)
1/4 cup pine nuts
2 garlic cloves
1/4 cup grated Parmesan cheese
1/4 teaspoon salt
2 tablespoons olive oil

SHRIMP
1/4 cup (1/2 stick) butter
1/2 cup chopped onion
2 garlic cloves, minced
1/2 teaspoon basil
12 ounces fresh shrimp, peeled, deveined
3 tablespoons (or more) chicken broth
12 ounces farfalle or other pasta, cooked, drained
grated Parmesan cheese

TO PREPARE THE PESTO, combine the basil, spinach, pine nuts, garlic, cheese and salt in a food processor and process until minced. Pulse until the mixture forms a paste, scraping down the side of the bowl frequently. Add the olive oil in a fine stream, processing continuously until the mixture is of the consistency of soft butter.

TO PREPARE THE SHRIMP, melt the butter in a skillet over medium heat. Add the onion and garlic and sauté until tender. Add the basil and shrimp and sauté until the shrimp are cooked through and pink, stirring constantly. Stir in the chicken broth and simmer for 1 to 2 minutes.

Toss the pasta with the pesto in a bowl, adding additional chicken broth if necessary for the desired consistency.

To serve, spoon the pasta mixture onto serving plates and top with 3 or 4 shrimp. Sprinkle with cheese and garnish with chopped fresh basil.

Serves 4 to 6 *Photograph for this recipe appears on page 158.*

WINE SUGGESTION: *Soave*

Asian Noodles with Ginger and Cilantro Sauce

12 ounces fresh oriental-style water noodles or linguini
salt to taste
1 tablespoon sesame oil
2 1/2 tablespoons minced fresh gingerroot
1 small jalapeño chile, seeded
1 cup packed fresh cilantro leaves
1 tablespoon soy sauce
1 tablespoon rice vinegar
1 tablespoon creamy peanut butter
3 tablespoons (or more) chicken broth
2 tablespoons sesame oil
pepper to taste

Cook the noodles in a large saucepan of salted boiling water just until tender; drain. Rinse with cold water and drain well. Toss the noodles with 1 tablespoon sesame oil in a large bowl.

Drop the gingerroot and jalapeño through the feed tube of a food processor while it is running and process until minced. Add the cilantro, soy sauce, vinegar, peanut butter, chicken broth and 2 tablespoons sesame oil and process until the mixture is almost smooth, adding more chicken broth if necessary for the desired consistency.

Season the sauce with salt and pepper and toss with the noodles in a large bowl to serve.

Serves 4

Wine Suggestion: *Tokay Pinot Gris*

Helpful Hint

Sometimes in cooking there is the tendency to think that if a little tastes good, then more is better. This is not so with sesame oil. The old saying that a little goes a long way definitely holds true for sesame oil. The distinctive flavor can easily overpower any dish when too much is used.

NOODLES ROMANOFF

8 ounces uncooked egg noodles
1 cup farmer-style cottage cheese
2 cups sour cream
2 tablespoons butter, softened
1 tablespoon Worcestershire sauce
1 teaspoon garlic salt
1 teaspoon onion salt
1/2 teaspoon salt
1/4 teaspoon pepper
1 cup shredded Old English sharp cheese

Cook the noodles just until tender using the package directions; drain. Combine the noodles, cottage cheese, sour cream, butter, Worcestershire sauce, garlic salt, onion salt, salt and pepper in a large bowl and mix gently.

Spoon into a buttered 2-quart baking dish and sprinkle evenly with the Old English cheese. Bake at 350 degrees for 30 minutes.

Serves 8 to 10

PAPPARDELLE WITH ASPARAGUS AND LEMON

1 bunch pencil-thin asparagus
8 ounces uncooked pappardelle
1/4 cup lemon juice
2 tablespoons dry white wine
1/2 teaspoon salt
1 cup heavy cream
2 tablespoons grated lemon zest
1 tablespoon minced Italian parsley

Snap off the tough ends of the asparagus and slice each spear diagonally into 3 or 4 equal pieces. Bring enough water to cover the asparagus to a boil in a large saucepan. Add the asparagus and cook for 2 minutes or just until tender-crisp; drain. Rinse with cold water and drain.

Cook the pasta in a large saucepan of salted boiling water for 10 to 12 minutes or until al dente.

Combine the lemon juice and wine in a small nonstick skillet and cook over medium-high heat until reduced to 2 to 3 tablespoons. Stir in the salt and cream and cook until reduced to 2/3 cup, stirring occasionally. Remove from the heat and stir in half the lemon zest. Cover to keep warm.

Drain the pasta and combine with the asparagus, lemon sauce and parsley in the saucepan, tossing gently to combine. Spoon onto a serving platter and sprinkle with the remaining 1 tablespoon lemon zest.

Serves 6 to 8

HELPFUL HINT

This simple pasta dish is delicious when made with the wide noodles called pappardelle, but it is equally as good when prepared with the more readily available fettuccini.

Pasta with Fresh Herbs and Summer Vegetables

Tomato Sauce

2 small onions, finely chopped
6 tablespoons olive oil
2 tablespoons minced garlic
1 tablespoon minced fresh oregano
1 tablespoon minced fresh basil
1 tablespoon minced fresh parsley

1 bay leaf
12 to 20 fresh ripe tomatoes, peeled,
   seeded, chopped, or 2 to
   3 (16-ounce) cans whole peeled
   tomatoes
salt, pepper and sugar to taste

Vegetables and Pasta

1 pound eggplant, peeled, cut into
   1/2-inch cubes
salt to taste
1/4 cup (or more) olive oil
2 to 3 medium onions, chopped
3 large garlic cloves, crushed
1 pound yellow squash, thinly sliced
1 pound zucchini, thinly sliced
1 each red, green and yellow bell
   pepper, chopped

1 bay leaf
2 or 3 sprigs each of parsley, basil
   and oregano
pepper to taste
sugar or tomato paste
1 pound large plum tomatoes,
   peeled, seeded, chopped, drained
24 to 32 ounces fresh angel hair
   pasta, linguini or spaghetti,
   cooked, drained

To prepare the sauce, sauté the onions in the olive oil in a large saucepan over medium-high heat until tender but not brown, stirring constantly. Add the garlic, oregano, basil, parsley and bay leaf and mix well. Add the tomatoes and cook over high heat until the liquid evaporates and the mixture is reduced to the desired consistency. Season with salt, pepper and sugar; set aside to cool.

To prepare the vegetables, soak the eggplant cubes in salted water to cover for 1 hour. Drain and pat dry with paper towels. Brown the eggplant in the olive oil in a wide saucepan over high heat, stirring constantly. Remove to paper towels with a slotted spoon.

Add additional olive oil to the saucepan if necessary. Sauté the onions and garlic in the oil over medium heat just until the vegetables begin to brown, stirring constantly. Add the yellow squash, zucchini, bell peppers, bay leaf, and sprigs of parsley, basil and oregano and toss to mix well. Cook just until tender-crisp. Season with salt and pepper. Add the tomatoes and sprinkle with sugar or stir in the tomato paste to adjust the acidity. Cook until thickened to the desired consistency, stirring constantly. Discard the bay leaf.

To serve, toss the sauce with the vegetables and pasta in a large serving bowl. Garnish with olives, thinly sliced prosciutto, grated Parmesan cheese and thinly sliced fresh basil.

Serves 4 to 6

Wine Suggestion: *Young Piedmontese Barbera*

TWO-CHEESE PENNE

TOMATO SAUCE
3 tablespoons olive oil
1 cup chopped onion
2 garlic cloves, minced
3 (28-ounce) cans Italian plum tomatoes
2 teaspoons basil
1 1/2 teaspoons crushed red pepper
2 cups reduced-sodium chicken broth
salt and black pepper to taste

PASTA
16 ounces uncooked penne
salt to taste
3 tablespoons olive oil
2 1/2 cups packed shredded Havarti cheese
1/3 cup grated Parmesan cheese

HELPFUL HINT

*The Tomato Sauce
in this recipe may
be prepared in
advance and
chilled, covered,
for up to 2 days.
Reheat it over
low heat before
proceeding with
the recipe. The
sauce can be used
in other dishes
as well.*

TO PREPARE THE TOMATO SAUCE, heat 3 tablespoons olive oil in a large heavy Dutch oven over medium-high heat. Add the onion and garlic and sauté for 5 minutes or until the onion is translucent.

Drain the tomatoes, reserving the liquid. Place the tomatoes in a food processor and pulse until chopped. Add the tomatoes, reserved liquid, basil, red pepper and broth to the onion mixture and bring to a boil, stirring constantly. Reduce the heat to medium and simmer for 1 hour and 10 minutes or until the mixture thickens and reduces to 6 cups, stirring occasionally. Season with salt and black pepper.

TO PREPARE THE PASTA, cook the pasta al dente in a large saucepan of salted boiling water. Drain and return the pasta to the saucepan. Add 3 tablespoons olive oil and toss to coat. Stir in the tomato sauce and toss with the Havarti cheese. Spoon into a baking dish and sprinkle evenly with the Parmesan cheese. Bake at 375 degrees for 30 minutes or until heated through.

Serves 8

WINE SUGGESTION: *Rosso di Montalcino or Chianti Classico*

PENNE À LA VODKA

2 tablespoons butter
2 tablespoons olive oil
1 medium onion, chopped
4 large garlic cloves, minced
24 mushrooms, sliced
2 bunches basil, chopped
20 Roma tomatoes, peeled, seeded, chopped
1/4 teaspoon crushed red pepper
salt and black pepper to taste
1/4 cup vodka
1/3 cup heavy cream
16 ounces penne, cooked, drained
1/4 cup grated Parmesan cheese

Heat the butter and olive oil in a large sauté pan over medium heat until the butter melts. Add the onion and garlic and sauté lightly. Add the mushrooms and sauté for 5 minutes, stirring constantly. Add the basil, tomatoes, red pepper, salt and black pepper and mix well. Simmer for 15 minutes, stirring occasionally. Add the vodka and simmer for 3 minutes longer.

Pour the mixture into a food processor and process until well combined. Stir in the cream.

Pour over the penne in a serving bowl and sprinkle with the cheese; garnish with additional chopped fresh basil.

You may add sautéed shrimp and scallops for a heartier meal.

Serves 4

WINE SUGGESTION: *California Sangiovese*

TOASTED ROTINI WITH WILD MUSHROOM SAUCE

WILD MUSHROOM SAUCE
1/4 cup olive oil
1 pound wild mushrooms or white button mushrooms, sliced
2 garlic cloves, minced
1 teaspoon oregano
1 teaspoon basil
1/4 cup chopped parsley
1/2 cup white wine or chicken broth

TOASTED ROTINI
1/4 cup (or more) olive oil
16 ounces uncooked rotini
1 (14-ounce) can (or more) chicken broth
1/4 cup cream or milk
1/4 cup grated Parmesan cheese

TO PREPARE THE SAUCE, heat the olive oil in a heavy saucepan over medium-high heat. Add the mushrooms and sauté for 2 minutes. Add the garlic, oregano, basil and parsley and sauté for 1 minute, stirring constantly. Stir in the wine and cook for 1 to 3 minutes or until of the desired consistency. Spoon into a bowl.

TO PREPARE THE ROTINI, heat the olive oil in the same saucepan over medium-high heat. Add the pasta and toast for 10 minutes or until golden brown, stirring constantly and adjusting the temperature if the pasta begins to overbrown. Stir in the chicken broth and simmer until pasta is al dente, adding more broth if necessary.

Add the mushroom sauce and simmer until heated through. Stir in the cream and cheese and remove from the heat. Serve immediately.

Do not use flavored or colored pasta in this recipe.

Serves 4 to 6

WINE SUGGESTION: *Lightly-oaked Pinot*

VEGETABLE MANICOTTI

2 cups nonfat ricotta cheese
1/2 cup wheat germ
2 egg whites, lightly beaten
1/3 cup chopped parsley
2 tablespoons grated Parmesan cheese
3/4 teaspoon Italian seasoning
1/2 teaspoon salt
5 ounces manicotti, cooked
2/3 cup sliced yellow squash
2/3 cup sliced zucchini
2/3 cup sliced mushrooms
1 (28-ounce) jar spaghetti sauce
1/2 cup water

Combine the ricotta cheese, wheat germ, egg whites, parsley, Parmesan cheese, Italian seasoning and salt in a large bowl and mix well. Stuff each manicotti with the mixture, using a spoon or pastry bag.

Arrange the stuffed manicotti in a single layer in a 9×13-inch baking dish sprayed with nonstick cooking spray. Top with the yellow squash, zucchini and mushrooms.

Mix the spaghetti sauce and water in a medium bowl and pour over the vegetables. Bake, covered with foil, at 350 degrees for 40 to 45 minutes or until the vegetables are tender and the cheeses are bubbling. Garnish with Parmesan cheese.

Serves 6

WINE SUGGESTION: *Chianti or Chianti Classico*

POLENTA GRATIN WITH SALSA ROJA

SALSA ROJA
3/4 cup chopped onion
1 tablespoon olive oil
4 garlic cloves, chopped
1/2 teaspoon cumin

1 (16-ounce) can tomatoes, chopped
2 teaspoons minced canned chipotle
    chiles in adobo sauce
salt and pepper to taste

POLENTA
4 1/2 cups water
1/2 teaspoon salt
cayenne pepper to taste

1 cup yellow cornmeal
2/3 cup shredded Cheddar cheese
salt and black pepper to taste

VEGETABLES
3 1/2 cups sliced mushrooms
2 garlic cloves, minced
1/4 teaspoon cumin
1 tablespoon olive oil
1 medium zucchini, sliced

1 jalapeño chile, sliced
2 tablespoons minced fresh cilantro
1/8 teaspoon cayenne pepper
1 1/2 cups lightly packed shredded
    Cheddar cheese

TO PREPARE THE SALSA, sauté the onion in the heated olive oil in a heavy medium saucepan over medium heat for 6 minutes or until tender. Add the garlic and cumin and sauté for 1 minute. Stir in the undrained tomatoes and chipotles and simmer for 30 minutes or until thickened, stirring occasionally. Season with salt and pepper.

TO PREPARE THE POLENTA, bring the water, 1/2 teaspoon salt and cayenne pepper to a boil in a large heavy saucepan. Whisk in the cornmeal and bring the mixture back to a boil, whisking constantly. Reduce the heat to low and cook for 30 minutes or until very thick, stirring occasionally. Remove from the heat and stir in the cheese, salt and black pepper. Spoon into a 9×13-inch baking dish lightly brushed with olive oil; cool.

TO PREPARE THE VEGETABLES, sauté the mushrooms, garlic and cumin in the heated olive oil in a large heavy skillet over medium-high heat for 7 minutes or until the mushrooms are golden brown. Reduce the heat to medium and add the zucchini and jalapeño. Cook for 5 minutes or until the zucchini is tender-crisp, stirring occasionally. Remove from the heat and add the cilantro and cayenne pepper.

Cut the cooled polenta into 3-inch squares. Cut each square diagonally into 2 triangles. Spread the salsa evenly in a 9×13-inch baking dish. Arrange the polenta triangles in slightly overlapping rows in the prepared dish. Spoon the vegetable mixture evenly over the polenta and sprinkle with the cheese. Bake, covered, at 375 degrees for 30 minutes.

Serves 6

WINE SUGGESTION: *Dry Riesling*

GNOCCHI

4 cups milk
1/2 cup (1 stick) butter, softened
1 cup uncooked grits
1 teaspoon salt
pepper to taste

1/3 cup butter, melted
1 cup shredded New York white
    Cheddar or Gruyère cheese
1/3 cup grated Parmesan cheese

Bring the milk to a boil in a large saucepan over medium-high heat. Add 1/2 cup butter and stir until the butter melts. Add the grits gradually, stirring constantly. Bring the mixture to a boil and cook until the mixture thickens, stirring constantly. Remove from the heat and season with the salt and pepper.

Spoon into a mixing bowl and beat at high speed for 5 minutes. Pour into a shallow 9×13-inch dish and chill in the refrigerator. Cut into rectangles and arrange in an overlapping layer in a buttered baking dish. Pour 1/3 cup melted butter evenly over the top and sprinkle with the cheeses. Refrigerate, covered, until 1 hour before serving time. Let stand at room temperature for 30 minutes. Bake at 400 degrees for 30 to 35 minutes or until light brown. Cool slightly and serve with beef tenderloin.

Serves 5 to 8

BARLEY PILAF

1 tablespoon olive oil
1 large red bell pepper, chopped
2 bunches green onions, chopped
1 1/2 cups pearl barley
2 (14-ounce) cans vegetable or
   chicken broth

2 cups frozen corn
1/2 cup sliced fresh basil
salt and pepper to taste

Heat the olive oil in a heavy medium saucepan over medium-high heat. Add the bell pepper and half the green onions and sauté for 5 minutes or until tender. Add the barley and stir until coated with the olive oil. Add the broth and bring the mixture to a boil, stirring constantly. Reduce the heat and simmer, covered, for 40 minutes or until the barley is tender, stirring occasionally. Add the corn and cook for 5 minutes or until heated through, stirring occasionally. Stir in the basil and remaining 1 bunch green onions. Season with salt and pepper.

Serves 6

WINE SUGGESTION: *Pinot Grigio*

WILD RICE WITH MUSHROOMS

1/2 cup wild rice (about 4 ounces)
2 cups reduced-sodium chicken broth
6 tablespoons (3/4 stick) butter
1 pound mushrooms, sliced
1 teaspoon crumbled rosemary
1/4 teaspoon rubbed sage
cayenne pepper to taste
1/4 cup dry sherry
salt and black pepper to taste

Combine the rice and chicken broth in a heavy medium saucepan. Simmer, covered, over low heat for 1 hour or until the rice is tender and the broth is absorbed. Remove from the heat.

Melt the butter in a heavy large skillet over medium-high heat. Add the mushrooms, rosemary, sage and cayenne pepper and sauté for 12 minutes or until the mushrooms are golden brown. Add the sherry and cook for 2 minutes or until the liquid is evaporated, scraping any browned bits from the bottom of the skillet and stirring constantly.

Stir in the rice. Cook for 2 minutes or until heated through. Season with salt and black pepper. Serve with chicken or game.

Serves 4

ARTICHOKE RISOTTO

1^1/$_2$ cups beef broth
1^1/$_2$ cups water
1^1/$_2$ tablespoons olive oil
1 tablespoon butter
^{1}/$_2$ cup finely chopped onion
1 cup sliced drained artichoke hearts
2 teaspoons minced garlic
1 cup uncooked arborio rice
^{1}/$_4$ cup dry white wine
salt and freshly ground pepper to taste
^{1}/$_4$ cup chopped fresh parsley
1 tablespoon butter
^{1}/$_4$ cup freshly grated Parmesan cheese

Combine the beef broth and water in a medium saucepan and simmer over low heat to keep warm.

Heat the olive oil and 1 tablespoon butter in a large heavy saucepan over low heat. Add the onion and cook for 7 minutes or until the onion is tender-crisp, stirring frequently. Stir in the artichokes and garlic and cook for 5 minutes longer or until the onion is tender. Add the rice and cook for 1 to 3 minutes or until the rice is opaque, stirring constantly. Add the wine and cook for 3 minutes or until the liquid is absorbed, stirring frequently.

Add ^{1}/$_2$ cup of the warm broth mixture and cook for 3 to 5 minutes or until most of the liquid is absorbed, stirring frequently. Season with salt and pepper. Add the remaining broth mixture ^{1}/$_2$ cup at a time, simmering until the liquid is absorbed after each addition and cooking until the rice is tender and creamy, stirring constantly; the cooking time will total 25 to 30 minutes. Remove from the heat and add the parsley, 1 tablespoon butter and cheese, mixing well. Serve immediately.

Serves 3 to 6

CARAMELIZED GARLIC RISOTTO

24 unpeeled garlic cloves
1 tablespoon olive oil
3 tablespoons unsalted butter
1 tablespoon olive oil
1 medium onion, minced
1 1/2 cups uncooked arborio rice or medium-grain rice
1/2 cup dry white wine
5 cups chicken stock or canned reduced-sodium chicken broth
1/2 cup chopped fresh chives or green onions
salt and pepper to taste

Bring a medium saucepan of water to a boil over high heat.
Add the garlic and cook for 30 seconds; drain. Repeat the process
using fresh water; drain. Remove the garlic to a baking sheet and
drizzle with 1 tablespoon olive oil, tossing to coat. Bake at 350
degrees for 25 minutes or until golden brown. Cool, peel and chop
the garlic.

Melt the butter with 1 tablespoon olive oil in a heavy medium
skillet over medium-low heat. Add the onion and sauté for 5
minutes, stirring constantly. Add the rice and cook for 1 minute,
stirring constantly. Add the wine and simmer until the liquid is
almost absorbed, stirring frequently.

Stir in the chicken stock and simmer, uncovered, for 30 minutes
or until the rice is tender and the mixture is creamy, stirring
frequently. Stir in the garlic and chives and season with salt
and pepper.

You may prepare the garlic in advance and store, covered, in the
refrigerator for up to 1 day before using.

Serves 6

HELPFUL HINT

*Don't wash risotto
rice before cooking,
because it will lose
the starches vital to
the dish. Instead,
toast the rice in
olive oil or butter so
that each grain is
lightly coated. This
way, the rice will
absorb the cooking
liquid gradually
and release its
starches slowly,
which is the key
to achieving a
creamy risotto.*

SIDE DISHES

ARTICHOKE AND MUSHROOM PIE

OLD-FASHIONED PASTRY
2 cups flour
1 teaspoon salt

2/3 cup shortening
1/4 cup cold water

ARTICHOKE AND MUSHROOM FILLING
2 garlic cloves, minced
8 ounces fresh mushrooms, sliced
1 tablespoon olive oil
1 (14-ounce) can artichoke hearts,
    drained, sliced
4 eggs, lightly beaten

1 cup shredded mozzarella cheese
1 cup shredded Cheddar cheese
1 cup shredded Swiss cheese
1/4 cup chopped black olives
1/8 teaspoon pepper

TO PREPARE THE PASTRY, combine the flour and salt in a bowl. Cut in the shortening until crumbly. Add the water 1 tablespoon at a time, mixing with a pastry cutter until the mixture forms a ball. Shape into 2 equal discs and chill, wrapped in plastic, for 30 minutes or longer.

Roll 1 disc to fit a 9-inch deep-dish pie plate. Roll the remaining disc into a 10-inch circle for the top pastry.

TO PREPARE THE FILLING, sauté the garlic and mushrooms in the olive oil in a medium skillet over medium-high heat, stirring constantly. Add the artichoke hearts and mix well. Spoon into the pastry-lined pie plate.

Combine the eggs, cheeses, olives and pepper in a large bowl and mix well. Pour over the vegetables. Top with the remaining pastry; seal the edge and cut steam vents. Bake at 350 degrees for 40 to 50 minutes or until golden brown.

Serves 8

Frijoles à la Charra

1 1/2 cups dried pinto beans, sorted, rinsed
2 garlic bulbs
6 cups water
1/4 cup chopped onion
8 ounces kielbasa, thinly sliced, or 8 ounces chopped bacon
  (optional)
1 cup chopped tomato
7 serrano chiles, seeded, chopped
3/4 cup chopped cilantro
1 tablespoon tomato bouillon, or salt to taste

Combine the beans, garlic bulbs and water in a large heavy saucepan. Bring to a boil over high heat. Reduce the heat and simmer, covered, for 4 hours. Remove the garlic, leaving the beans to continue simmering over low heat.

Cook the onion and kielbasa in a nonstick skillet over medium heat until the onion is tender and the kielbasa is cooked through; drain. Add to the beans with the tomato, serranos, cilantro and bouillon and mix well. Cook for 15 minutes or until the beans are tender, stirring occasionally.

Serves 4

HELPFUL HINT

For a true Tex-Mex dinner, serve Frijoles à la Charra with cooked white rice, corn or flour tortillas and/or quesadillas and garnish with chopped avocado and fresh lime juice. In Mexico, beans are often prepared once a week and the leftovers reheated and mashed to make refried beans.

SZECHUAN SESAME BROCCOLI

HELPFUL HINT

*Szechuan cuisine
has a reputation for
its bold and
pungent flavors.
Traditional
Szechuan dishes
are often quite
spicy, but we've
given this recipe
only a slight dose
of heat. If your
taste runs more to
the fiery side, make
yours hotter by
adding more red
pepper flakes.*

2 teaspoons sesame seeds
1 1/2 tablespoons vegetable oil
1 teaspoon sesame oil
1 small onion, cut into wedges
2 garlic cloves, minced
2 tablespoons water
8 ounces broccoli, cut into 2- to 3-inch florets
1 (8-ounce) can sliced water chestnuts, drained
1 tablespoon soy sauce
2 teaspoons dry sherry
1/2 teaspoon ground or crushed red pepper

Toast the sesame seeds in a skillet over low heat for 5 minutes, stirring frequently; remove the sesame seeds and set aside. Add the vegetable oil and sesame oil to the skillet and heat. Add the onion, garlic, water and broccoli. Cook, covered, for 7 to 10 minutes or until the broccoli is tender-crisp, stirring occasionally.

Add the water chestnuts, soy sauce, sherry and red pepper and cook, uncovered, for 2 minutes, stirring occasionally. Remove to a serving dish and sprinkle with the toasted sesame seeds.

Serves 4

BROCCOLI AND CHEDDAR PIE IN POTATO CRUST

POTATO CRUST
2 cups packed grated peeled potato
1/2 teaspoon salt
1 egg
1/4 cup grated onion
vegetable oil

BROCCOLI AND CHEDDAR FILLING
1 cup chopped yellow onion
1 garlic clove, crushed
3 tablespoons butter
1/2 teaspoon basil
thyme and pepper to taste
1/2 teaspoon salt
1 medium head broccoli, broken into florets
1 1/2 cups packed shredded Cheddar cheese
2 eggs, beaten
1/4 cup milk
1 tablespoon vegetable oil
paprika to taste

HELPFUL HINT

For a quick and colorful side dish, prepare Confetti Broccoli. Steam broccoli with slivers of red and yellow bell peppers and toss with a lemon dressing.

TO PREPARE THE CRUST, sprinkle the grated potato with the salt and drain in a colander for 10 minutes. Press out the excess moisture. Combine the potato, egg and onion in a bowl and mix well. Press over the bottom and up the side of a 9-inch pie plate with lightly floured fingers. Bake at 400 degrees for 30 minutes. Remove and brush the entire surface of the crust lightly with vegetable oil to crisp it. Bake for 10 to 15 minutes longer or until brown. Reduce the oven temperature to 375 degrees.

TO PREPARE THE FILLING, sauté the onion and garlic in the butter in a large saucepan over medium-high heat for 5 minutes. Add the basil, thyme, pepper, salt and broccoli and cook, covered, for 10 minutes, stirring occasionally.

Sprinkle half the cheese into the baked crust and top with the sautéed vegetables. Top with the remaining cheese. Beat the eggs, milk, vegetable oil and pepper to taste in a small bowl. Pour over the layers and sprinkle the top with paprika. Bake at 375 degrees for 35 to 40 minutes or until set.

Serves 6 to 8

BRUSSELS SPROUTS WITH
MAPLE MUSTARD VINAIGRETTE

HELPFUL HINT

Brussels sprouts should be purchased loose with firm, tight, bright green heads. The smallest sprouts make the best eating. Discard the tougher outer leaves, as the slightly bitter taste associated with some Brussels sprouts is found there. Sprouts can be stored overnight in the refrigerator after being cooked. Reheat the sprouts in boiling water or in a microwave and drain to proceed with the recipe.

2 pounds Brussels sprouts
salt to taste
2 tablespoons white wine vinegar
2 tablespoons balsamic vinegar
2 tablespoons maple syrup
1 tablespoon coarse-grain mustard
$1/8$ teaspoon grated fresh nutmeg
$1/2$ cup olive oil
freshly ground pepper to taste

Trim the bottoms of the Brussels sprouts, discarding the outer leaves. Cut a $1/4$-inch-deep X in the stem end of each Brussels sprout to ensure even cooking. Bring a large saucepan of salted water to a boil over high heat. Add the Brussels sprouts and cook for 10 to 15 minutes or just until tender, stirring occasionally. Plunge the sprouts into ice water to stop the cooking process; drain.

Whisk the vinegars, maple syrup, mustard, nutmeg, olive oil, salt and pepper to taste in a small bowl until thick and smooth. Add the Brussels sprouts and toss to mix well.

The Brussels sprouts may be cooked and the vinaigrette prepared in advance. Reheat the sprouts in boiling water or in the microwave to toss with the vinaigrette.

Serves 4 to 6

Spiced Red Cabbage with Apples and Thyme

2 pounds red cabbage, cored, shredded
1 pound Granny Smith or other tart green apples, peeled, cored, finely chopped
1 large onion, finely chopped
2 garlic cloves, chopped
1/2 cup dry red wine
1/2 cup orange juice
2 tablespoons red wine vinegar
2 tablespoons dark brown sugar
1 tablespoon grated orange zest
1 teaspoon thyme
1/4 teaspoon cinnamon
1/4 teaspoon nutmeg
1/4 teaspoon allspice
salt and pepper to taste

Combine the cabbage, apples, onion, garlic, wine, orange juice, vinegar, brown sugar, orange zest, thyme, cinnamon, nutmeg and allspice in a large heavy Dutch oven and mix well.

Bake, covered, at 400 degrees for 1 hour or until the cabbage is tender. Remove the Dutch oven to the stovetop and cook, uncovered, for 5 minutes or until the liquid thickens slightly, stirring frequently. Season with salt and pepper and serve as a colorful accompaniment to roast pork or game.

Serves 8

In 1916, Tulsan Josh Cosden earned the nickname "Prince of Petroleum" when, in the lobby of the Hotel Tulsa, he nonchalantly wrote a twelve-million-dollar check to buy the Hill Oil Company.

Carrot Loaf

1/4 cup (1/2 stick) butter
2 pounds carrots, peeled, cut into
  1/4-inch pieces
2 tablespoons butter
4 ounces mushrooms, sliced
1/2 cup chopped onion
2 garlic cloves, minced

5 eggs, beaten
4 ounces Swiss cheese, shredded
1 teaspoon salt
1 teaspoon pepper
2 tablespoons butter
8 ounces spinach, stems removed

Melt 1/4 cup butter in a sauté pan over medium-high heat. Add the carrots and sauté until tender. Remove the carrots to a large bowl and cut into smaller pieces. Melt 2 tablespoons butter in the same pan and add the mushrooms, onion and garlic and sauté for 2 minutes. Add to the carrots.

Combine the eggs and cheese in a medium bowl and mix well. Add to the carrot mixture. Add the salt and pepper and mix well. Melt 2 tablespoons butter in the same pan and add the spinach. Sauté until the spinach wilts. Remove and chop the spinach.

Spread half the carrot mixture evenly in a 5×9-inch loaf pan lined with greased foil. Top with the spinach and spread the remaining carrot mixture over the spinach. Place the loaf pan in a larger pan and fill the larger pan with warm water to a depth of 1 inch. Bake at 400 degrees for 1 1/4 hours or until a knife inserted in the center comes out clean. Cool slightly. Invert onto a serving platter and remove the foil. Slice to serve.

Serves 6 to 8

Orange-Glazed Carrots

2 pounds baby carrots
2 tablespoons sugar
2 1/2 teaspoons cornstarch
1/2 teaspoon salt

1/2 teaspoon ginger
1/2 cup orange juice
2 tablespoons margarine

Cook the carrots in water to cover in a saucepan for 8 minutes or until tender; drain. Remove to a serving dish and keep warm.

Whisk the sugar, cornstarch, salt and ginger in a small saucepan. Add the orange juice gradually, whisking constantly. Bring the mixture to a boil over high heat and boil for 1 minute, stirring constantly. Add the margarine, stirring until melted and smooth. Pour over the carrots and mix to coat well.

Serves 8

BIXBY GRILLED CORN

6 to 8 ears of corn, shucked
6 to 8 tablespoons butter or margarine, melted
Creole seasoning to taste
salt and pepper to taste

Place each ear of corn on a 12×12-inch piece of foil. Drizzle 1 tablespoon of the melted butter over each ear of corn. Sprinkle with the Creole seasoning, salt and pepper and turn the ears of corn to coat well.

Seal the foil tightly around each ear of corn. Grill over hot coals for 10 to 15 minutes on each side or until done to taste.

Serves 6 to 8

HELPFUL HINT

The Green Corn Festival is held annually in Bixby the last weekend in June.

CORN PUDDING

1 (20-ounce) can cream-style corn
1 small green bell pepper, chopped
1 small onion, chopped
1 teaspoon Beau Monde seasoning
salt and pepper to taste
2 eggs, beaten
3/4 cup soft bread crumbs
3/4 cup shredded Cheddar cheese
2 slices bacon, crisp-fried, crumbled

Combine the corn, bell pepper, onion, seasoning, salt, pepper, eggs and bread crumbs in a medium bowl and mix well. Spoon into a greased 2-quart baking dish and sprinkle evenly with the cheese and bacon. Bake at 325 degrees for 45 minutes.

Serves 6 to 8

OIL BARON'S SAUTÉED MUSHROOMS

HELPFUL HINT

Porcini mushrooms have a rich, meaty flavor. Also known by the French term "cèpes," they are available fresh or dried. When selecting fresh porcini, look for firm, plump mushrooms that are not slimy or bruised.

Cremini mushrooms, similar in size and shape to common cultivated white mushrooms, have a more pronounced flavor and a rich brown skin concealing creamy tan flesh. Select firm, plump mushrooms.

1/2 cup (1 stick) unsalted butter
1 medium yellow onion, finely chopped
6 garlic cloves, minced
4 portobello mushroom caps, cut into 1/4-inch slices
2 teaspoons kosher salt
2 teaspoons pepper
1/4 cup Worcestershire sauce
1/4 cup Kitchen Bouquet
1 cup sour cream

Melt the butter in a large skillet over low heat. Add the onion and cook over low heat until caramelized, stirring occasionally. Add the garlic, mushrooms, salt and pepper and mix well. Cook over low to medium heat for 15 minutes, stirring occasionally.

Stir in the Worcestershire sauce and Kitchen Bouquet and cook for 5 minutes longer. Stir in the sour cream and cook, covered, for 2 minutes.

Serves 4 to 6

Wild Mushroom Tart

Tart Crust

1¹/4 cups flour
¹/2 teaspoon salt
¹/2 cup (1 stick) unsalted butter,
    chilled, cut into pieces

2 tablespoons ice water

Tart

1 cup water
1 ounce dried porcini mushrooms
¹/4 cup (¹/2 stick) unsalted butter
10 ounces cremini or button
    mushrooms, sliced
salt to taste
¹/4 cup minced shallots

2 tablespoons Cognac or brandy
2 tablespoons chopped mixed fresh
    herbs
²/3 cup shredded Gruyère cheese
³/4 cup heavy cream
2 egg yolks
1 egg

TO PREPARE THE CRUST, combine the flour and salt in a food processor. Add the butter and pulse until the mixture resembles coarse meal. Add the ice water 1 tablespoon at a time, pulsing until the mixture forms a ball. Flatten the dough into a disk and chill, wrapped in plastic wrap, for 45 minutes. Roll into a 12-inch circle on a floured surface. Fit into a 9-inch tart pan with removeable bottom. Trim the edge, leaving a ¹/2-inch overhang. Fold the overhang inward to form a thick edge and press the edge to raise the dough ¹/8 inch above the pan. Chill for 30 minutes. Line the pastry shell with foil and fill with dried beans. Bake at 375 degrees for 15 minutes. Remove the beans and foil and bake for 15 minutes longer or until golden brown.

TO PREPARE THE TART, bring the water to a boil in a saucepan. Add the porcini and remove from the heat. Let stand for 30 minutes. Drain and coarsely chop the porcini; reserving the soaking liquid. Strain the reserved liquid.

Melt the butter in a heavy large saucepan over high heat. Add the porcini mushooms, cremini mushrooms and salt. Sauté for 10 minutes or until the mushrooms are deep golden brown. Add the shallots and sauté for 2 minutes. Stir in the Cognac and reserved liquid. Bring the mixture to a boil and boil for 3 minutes or until most of the liquid is reduced. Stir in half the herbs and set aside to cool.

Sprinkle half the cheese over the prepared crust and layer the mushroom mixture evenly over the cheese. Whisk the cream, egg yolks, egg and remaining herbs in a bowl. Pour over the mushroom mixture and top with the remaining cheese. Bake at 375 degrees for 30 minutes or until set and golden brown. Cool on a wire rack for 15 minutes.

Serves 6

HEAVENLY ONIONS

6 large yellow or Vidalia onions, thinly sliced
6 tablespoons (3/4 stick) butter
1 pound Colby Jack cheese, shredded
1 (10-ounce) can cream of mushroom or cream of chicken soup
1 soup can heavy cream
1 tablespoon soy sauce
1/2 teaspoon pepper
8 slices French bread, buttered on both sides

Sauté the onions in the butter in a large sauté pan over medium-high heat until tender, stirring constantly. Remove to a 9×13-inch glass baking dish and sprinkle with the cheese. Combine the soup, cream, soy sauce and pepper in a medium bowl and whisk until well mixed. Pour over the cheese. Arrange the buttered bread over the top. Bake at 350 degrees for 30 to 40 minutes or until golden brown and bubbly.

Serves 6 to 8

ONION PIE

1 cup finely crushed saltine cracker crumbs
1/4 cup (1/2 stick) butter, melted
2 medium onions, thinly sliced, separated into rings
2 tablespoons butter, softened
3/4 cup milk
2 eggs, beaten, or an equivalent amount of egg substitute
1/2 teaspoon salt
pepper to taste
1/4 cup shredded Cheddar cheese
1/8 to 1/4 teaspoon paprika

Combine the cracker crumbs and 1/4 cup melted butter in a small bowl and mix well. Press over the bottom and up the side of a greased 8-inch pie plate. Sauté the onions in 2 tablespoons butter in a large skillet over medium-high heat until tender and golden brown. Spoon into the prepared pie plate. Combine the milk, eggs, salt and pepper in a small bowl and mix well. Pour over the onions. Sprinkle evenly with the cheese and paprika. Bake at 350 degrees for 30 minutes or until a knife inserted halfway between the center and edge comes out clean. Cool slightly before serving.

Serves 8

MASHED POTATOES WITH GARLIC AND PARMESAN CHEESE

1 pound boiling potatoes, peeled, cut into 1-inch pieces
1 teaspoon minced garlic
3 tablespoons butter
1/2 cup milk
1/3 cup grated Parmesan cheese
salt and pepper to taste

Cook the potatoes in water to cover in a saucepan until tender; drain. Remove the potatoes to a large bowl and mash by hand or with a hand mixer.

Sauté the garlic in the butter in a small saucepan over medium heat until the butter melts. Add the milk and heat just to the simmering point. Pour over the potatoes and stir to mix well. Mix in the cheese, salt and pepper; potatoes should be fluffy but not stiff.

Serves 4

POTATOES WITH GORGONZOLA CHEESE

2 1/2 pounds small red-skinned potatoes, cut into halves
3/4 tablespoon olive oil
1 teaspoon salt
1/2 teaspoon pepper
1 cup sour cream
6 ounces Gorgonzola cheese, crumbled, at room temperature
1/4 teaspoon Tabasco sauce
1/2 teaspoon pepper
10 to 12 slices bacon, crisp-fried, crumbled
1/3 cup walnuts, toasted, chopped
1/4 cup minced chives

Toss the potatoes with the olive oil, salt and 1/2 teaspoon pepper in a large bowl. Arrange in a single layer in a roasting pan. Roast at 400 degrees for 30 minutes or until tender and light brown. Remove to a serving dish.

Combine the sour cream and cheese in a small bowl and mix well. Add the Tabasco sauce and 1/2 teaspoon pepper and mix well. Stir in the bacon and walnuts. Spoon over the potatoes and sprinkle with the chives.

Serves 6 to 8

POTATOES AND GREEN BEANS WITH BLEU CHEESE AND WALNUTS

2 pounds small red-skinned
  potatoes, cut into quarters
8 tablespoons Mustard Vinaigrette
  (page 144)
1/3 cup crumbled bleu cheese

salt and pepper to taste
8 ounces thin green beans
3 tablespoons crumbled bleu cheese
1/3 cup chopped walnuts, toasted

Combine the potatoes with 3 tablespoons of the Mustard Vinaigrette in a large baking dish, tossing to coat. Roast at 450 degrees for 20 minutes. Reduce the oven temperature to 375 degrees and roast for 50 minutes longer or until the potatoes are tender, stirring occasionally. Cool slightly.

Combine 3 tablespoons of the Mustard Vinaigrette with 1/3 cup cheese in a medium bowl, stirring to mix. Season with salt and pepper. Add to the potatoes and mix gently. Remove to a serving dish.

Combine the beans with water to cover in a saucepan and bring to a boil. Cook for 7 minutes or until tender-crisp; drain. Remove to a medium bowl and add 3 tablespoons cheese, 2 tablespoons of the Mustard Vinaigrette and walnuts, tossing to coat. Spoon the green bean mixture over the potatoes. Serve as an accompaniment to Roasted Chicken with Mustard Vinaigrette (page 144). The Mustard Vinaigrette yields enough for both recipes.

Serves 4

PICNIC POTATOES

1 (2-pound) package frozen hash
  brown potatoes
1 (10-ounce) can cream of chicken
  soup
2 cups sour cream

1/2 cup (1 stick) margarine, melted
8 ounces shredded sharp cheese
1 cup chopped onion
1 cup crushed corn flakes

Thaw the potatoes for 30 minutes. Combine the potatoes with the soup, sour cream, margarine, cheese and onion in a large bowl and mix well. Spoon into a 9×13-inch nonstick baking pan and sprinkle evenly with the corn flakes. Bake at 375 degrees for 1 hour.

Serves 10

SPINACH ON ARTICHOKE BOTTOMS WITH HOLLANDAISE

SOUR CREAM HOLLANDAISE
1/2 cup sour cream
1/2 cup mayonnaise

2 tablespoons lemon juice

FILLED ARTICHOKE BOTTOMS
8 ounces fresh mushrooms
6 tablespoons (3/4 stick) butter
1 tablespoon flour
1/2 cup milk
1/8 teaspoon garlic powder

1/2 teaspoon salt
2 (10-ounce) packages frozen
    chopped spinach, cooked, drained
14 to 20 drained canned artichoke
    bottoms

TO PREPARE THE HOLLANDAISE, combine the sour cream, mayonnaise and lemon juice in a small saucepan and mix well. Warm over low heat until heated through. Keep warm.

TO PREPARE THE FILLED ARTICHOKE BOTTOMS, separate the mushroom caps and stems and reserve 1 mushroom cap for each artichoke bottom. Chop the remaining mushroom caps and stems. Sauté the chopped mushrooms in 2 tablespoons of the butter in a sauté pan over medium-high heat. Remove to a small bowl and set aside. Sauté the reserved mushroom caps in half the remaining butter in the same pan until tender. Set aside.

Melt the remaining 2 tablespoons butter in a medium saucepan and whisk in the flour until smooth. Add the milk gradually and cook until thick and bubbly, stirring constantly. Add the garlic powder and salt and mix well. Stir in the sautéed chopped mushrooms and spinach.

To serve, arrange the artichoke bottoms on a serving platter and top with the hot spinach mixture. Spoon the warm Hollandaise over the spinach and top with 1 sautéed mushroom cap.

This dish can be prepared 1 day ahead and reheated in a 375-degree oven for 15 minutes before serving.

Serves 7 to 10

LAYERED SPINACH AND RADICCHIO CREPES

HELPFUL HINT

To make individual servings of the Layered Spinach and Radicchio Crepes, layer 3 heaping tablespoons of the Radicchio Filling on one quarter of each crepe. Place 2 tablespoons of the spinach on an adjoining quarter of the crepes. Fold the empty halves over the filled halves.

Spread 1 1/2 tablespoons of the Gorgonzola Sauce over each folded crepe and sprinkle with 1 1/2 tablespoons of the mozzarella cheese and 1 1/2 teaspoons of the Parmesan cheese. Fold the crepes in half again, creating large triangles.

(continued on following page)

CREPES

2 eggs
1 egg yolk
2 cups milk

1 cup flour
butter

RADICCHIO FILLING

3 tablespoons olive oil
2 garlic cloves, minced
3 heads radicchio, minced

3/4 cup red wine
1 tablespoon drained capers

GORGONZOLA SAUCE

3 tablespoons butter
1/4 cup flour
2 cups milk
1/2 teaspoon salt

1/8 teaspoon pepper
1/8 teaspoon nutmeg
4 ounces Gorgonzola cheese, crumbled

SPINACH AND CHEESE LAYERS

12 ounces baby spinach, sautéed until wilted
2 cups shredded mozzarella cheese

1 cup freshly grated Parmesan cheese

TO PREPARE THE CREPES, whisk the eggs, egg yolk and 1/2 cup of the milk in a medium bowl. Add the flour and whisk until well combined. Add the remaining milk and whisk until completely smooth. Chill for 30 minutes.

Melt 1/2 teaspoon butter in a nonstick crepe pan or 8- or 9-inch nonstick skillet. Pour a scant 1/4 cup batter into the crepe pan and swirl to evenly coat the surface of the pan. Cook for 1 minute or until the crepe pulls away from the side of the pan. Turn and cook the other side for 1 minute. Repeat the process with the remaining crepe batter, adding butter to the pan as needed. Stack the cooked crepes between sheets of waxed paper.

TO PREPARE THE FILLING, heat the olive oil in a large sauté pan over medium-high heat. Add the garlic and radicchio and cook for 5 minutes, stirring to cook evenly. Add the wine and reduce the heat to medium. Cook until the wine has evaporated. Add the capers and cook for 3 minutes, stirring frequently. Remove to a bowl.

TO PREPARE THE SAUCE, melt the butter in a medium saucepan over medium heat. Stir in the flour and cook for 1 minute, stirring constantly. Stir in the milk gradually and add the salt, pepper and nutmeg. Cook for 10 minutes or until the mixture is thickened, whisking constantly. Add the cheese and cook until melted, stirring constantly.

To assemble, place 2 crepes side by side in a buttered 9×13-inch glass baking dish. Spread the crepes with 1 cup of the Radicchio Filling and 2/3 cup of the Gorgonzola Sauce.

Layer with 2 additional crepes, 1 cup of the spinach, 1/4 cup of the mozzarella cheese and 1/4 cup of the Parmesan cheese.

Layer with 2 additional crepes, 1 cup of the mozzarella cheese and 1/2 cup of the Parmesan cheese.

Layer with 2 additional crepes, half the remaining Radicchio Filling and half the remaining Gorgonzola Sauce.

Layer with 2 additional crepes, the remaining spinach, 1/4 cup of the mozzarella cheese and the remaining Parmesan cheese.

Layer with 2 additional crepes, the remaining Radicchio Filling, Gorgonzola Sauce and mozzarella cheese. Bake at 375 degrees for 20 minutes. Store any remaining crepes for another use.

Serves 12 to 14

Top each crepe with 1 scant tablespoon of the remaining Gorgonzola Sauce, 1 scant tablespoon of the mozzarella cheese and 1 1/2 teaspoons of the Parmesan cheese.

Carefully remove completed crepes to a buttered baking sheet with a spatula. Bake as directed for the layered crepes and carefully transfer to serving dishes.

Spinach and Red Pepper Timbales with Peas

Helpful Hint

A timbale is a custard mixture baked in an individual mold called a timbale mold. You may substitute custard cups for the specialized molds in this recipe. The timbales bake in a water bath which insulates for more even cooking.

1 (10-ounce) package frozen spinach, thawed
1 large red bell pepper, chopped
1 tablespoon unsalted butter
1 (10-ounce) package frozen peas, thawed, drained
3/4 cup chicken broth
1 teaspoon chervil
1 tablespoon sugar
salt and freshly ground pepper to taste
3 eggs, lightly beaten

Drain the spinach, pressing out the excess moisture. Sauté the bell pepper in the butter in a small skillet over medium-high heat until tender, stirring constantly; cool.

Combine the bell pepper with the spinach, peas, broth, chervil, sugar, salt and pepper in a food processor or blender and process to mix well. Add the eggs and process until smooth.

Spoon into 8 buttered 1/2-cup timbale molds or custard cups. Arrange the molds in a large baking pan and fill the pan with hot water to halfway up the sides of the molds. Bake at 400 degrees for 35 minutes or until a knife inserted in the center comes out clean. Invert onto serving plates to serve.

This may be prepared 1 day ahead and chilled. Unmold the timbales into a glass dish just large enough to hold them and add 2 tablespoons water to the dish. Bake, covered with foil, at 500 degrees for 15 minutes.

Serves 8

Minted Sugar Snap Peas and Pearl Onions

1 pint pearl onions
2 pounds sugar snap peas, strings removed
$^1/_4$ cup ($^1/_2$ stick) unsalted butter
$^1/_4$ cup chopped fresh mint
salt and pepper to taste

Combine the onions with water to cover in a saucepan and cook for 7 minutes or until tender-crisp. Remove the onions to a bowl of ice water with a slotted spoon.

Return the water in the saucepan to a boil. Add the peas and cook for 3 minutes or until tender-crisp; drain. Add the peas to the ice water to cool. Drain the onions and the peas and peel the onions.

Heat the butter in a large heavy skillet over medium-high heat for 2 minutes or until the butter is brown. Add the onions, peas and mint and sauté for 1 minute or until heated through. Season with salt and pepper.

Serves 10

HELPFUL HINT

Brown butter refers to butter that is cooked over low heat until light hazelnut in color. This gives the butter a rich flavor that marries well with the crisp fresh flavor of the snap peas and onions.

Whipped Sweet Potatoes with Cardamom

$4^3/_4$ pounds sweet potatoes, cooked, peeled
1 cup (2 sticks) butter, softened
$^3/_4$ cup cream, heated
1 teaspoon cardamom
$^1/_4$ teaspoon nutmeg
salt to taste

Whip the potatoes in a large bowl until fluffy. Add the butter, cream, cardamom and nutmeg and beat until smooth and creamy. Season with salt. Spoon into a greased 9×13-inch baking pan and smooth the top with a spatula. Bake at 350 degrees for 45 minutes or until heated through and just beginning to brown.

Serves 8

HELPFUL HINT

A member of the ginger family, cardamom is a sweet, exotic-tasting spice. The small, round seeds, which grow inside husk-like pods the size of cranberries, are best purchased whole. They can be ground in a spice grinder or in a mortar with a pestle.

SWEET POTATO SOUFFLÉ

HELPFUL HINT

For variety, try Oatmeal Crunch Topping on a sweet potato casserole. Process 3 cups broken crisp oatmeal cookies in a food processor until fine. Add 6 tablespoons cold unsalted butter pieces and pulse until the mixture resembles soft cookie dough. Wrap in waxed paper and chill for 2 hours or until firm. Crumble the topping over the casserole and bake until golden brown. The topping may be made 1 day ahead, covered and chilled until needed.

4 medium sweet potatoes, cooked, peeled
$1/3$ stick butter
1 cup sugar
2 eggs
$1/2$ cup milk
1 teaspoon vanilla extract
$1^1/2$ teaspoons cinnamon
1 cup packed brown sugar
$1/2$ to 1 cup chopped nuts
$1/3$ cup flour
$1/3$ stick butter

Combine the potatoes, $1/3$ stick butter, sugar, eggs, milk, vanilla and cinnamon in a mixing bowl and beat until light and fluffy. Spoon into a buttered soufflé dish.

Combine the brown sugar, nuts, flour and $1/3$ stick butter in a medium bowl and mix until crumbly. Sprinkle evenly over the sweet potatoes. Bake at 350 degrees for 40 to 45 minutes or until golden brown and bubbly.

Serves 6

ZUCCHINI AND TOMATO SKILLET

1 onion, chopped
1/4 cup (1/2 stick) butter, melted
4 medium zucchini, sliced
4 ounces fresh mushrooms, sliced
3 medium tomatoes, sliced
3 tablespoons chopped fresh parsley
1/2 teaspoon dried basil, or 1 1/2 tablespoons chopped fresh basil
1/4 teaspoon salt
1/4 teaspoon coarsely ground pepper
1/8 teaspoon garlic powder
1/4 cup grated Parmesan cheese
1 cup shredded Cheddar cheese

Sauté the onion in the butter in a large skillet over medium-high heat until tender, stirring constantly. Add the zucchini and mushrooms and cook for 5 minutes or until the zucchini is tender-crisp, stirring frequently. Add the tomatoes and cook for 1 minute, stirring frequently.

Drain the vegetables and return them to the skillet. Stir in the parsley, basil, salt, pepper, garlic powder and Parmesan cheese gently. Cook for 1 minute or until heated through. Remove from the heat and sprinkle with the Cheddar cheese. Let stand, covered, for 3 to 5 minutes or until the cheese melts. Serve immediately.

Serves 6

In the 1930s, Tulsa was called the city "with the atmosphere of Lower Manhattan and the style of Fifth Avenue, with more millionaires in one generation than grew in New England in a century."

DESSERTS

CHEESECAKE

HELPFUL HINT

*This cheesecake
can also be made
with a Zwieback
Crust. Mix
18 crushed
zwieback with
1/2 cup melted
butter, 1/4 cup
sugar and 1 teaspoon
cinnamon in a
bowl. Reserve some
of the crumbs to
sprinkle over
the top of the
cheesecake and
proceed as for
the graham
cracker crust.*

GRAHAM CRACKER CRUST
22 single graham crackers, crushed
1/2 cup (1 stick) butter, melted
cinnamon to taste

FILLING
16 ounces cream cheese, softened
2 eggs
1 cup sugar
1 tablespoon vanilla extract

SOUR CREAM TOPPING
12 ounces sour cream
3/4 cup sugar
2 tablespoons vanilla extract
1 teaspoon cinnamon
2 tablespoons sugar

FOR THE CRUST, mix the graham cracker crumbs, melted butter
and cinnamon in a bowl. Press firmly over the bottom of a round
8-inch springform pan. Bake at 350 degrees for 6 minutes. Cool
to room temperature.

FOR THE FILLING, combine the cream cheese and eggs in a mixing
bowl and beat until smooth. Add the sugar and vanilla and mix
well. Pour into the crust and bake for 18 minutes or until set.

FOR THE TOPPING, mix the sour cream, 3/4 cup sugar and vanilla
in a mixing bowl. Spread over the cheesecake. Combine the
cinnamon and 2 tablespoons sugar in a small bowl. Sprinkle over
the sour cream mixture. Bake for 6 minutes longer.

Cool the cheesecake to room temperature on a wire rack. Store in
the refrigerator for 10 hours or longer. Place on a serving plate
and loosen the cheesecake from the side of the pan with a knife;
remove the side of the pan. Garnish as desired.

Serves 8 *Photograph for this recipe appears on page 206.*

PORTER PEACH COBBLER

COBBLER PASTRY
2 cups flour
1 teaspoon salt
2/3 cup shortening
3 to 4 tablespoons cold water

FILLING
8 cups sliced peeled fresh peaches or frozen peaches
1 1/4 cups sugar
1/3 cup packed brown sugar
1/4 cup flour
1 teaspoon vanilla extract
1 teaspoon grated lemon zest
1 teaspoon cinnamon
1/4 teaspoon ginger
1/3 cup margarine, melted

HELPFUL HINT

Porter, Oklahoma is the peach capital of Oklahoma. The annual festival, featuring a wide variety of peaches, is enjoyed by many every July.

TO PREPARE THE PASTRY, combine the flour with the salt in a medium bowl. Cut in the shortening until the mixture resembles coarse meal. Add the water 1 tablespoon at a time, mixing with a fork until the mixture forms a ball. Chill, wrapped in plastic wrap, for 30 minutes or longer.

TO PREPARE THE FILLING, combine the peaches, sugar, brown sugar, flour, vanilla, lemon zest, cinnamon and ginger in a large saucepan and toss to coat evenly. Bring the mixture to a boil, stirring constantly. Reduce the heat to low and cook until peaches are tender, stirring frequently. Remove from the heat and stir in the margarine. Spoon half the peaches into a greased 7×11-inch baking dish.

Roll half the dough 1/8 inch thick on a floured surface. Trim the edges to form a 7×11-inch rectangle. Place over the peaches. Bake at 475 degrees for 15 minutes.

Top with the remaining peach mixture. Roll the remaining dough 1/8 inch thick on a floured surface and cut into 1-inch strips. Arrange lattice-fashion over the peach mixture. Bake for 18 to 20 minutes longer or until golden brown.

Serves 8

Chocolate Custard Gems

Helpful Hint

To avoid raw eggs that may carry salmonella, you may substitute an equivalent amount of commercially pasteurized egg substitute for any recipe using uncooked eggs. Meringue powder, sometimes sold as powdered egg whites, may also be used.

1/2 cup (1 stick) butter, softened
1/4 cup packed brown sugar
3 tablespoons baking cocoa
1 egg, beaten
2 cups graham cracker crumbs
1 cup flaked coconut
1/2 cup chopped walnuts
2 cups confectioners' sugar
1/4 cup (1/2 stick) butter, softened
1/4 cup cream or milk
2 tablespoons Bird's custard powder
3 ounces semisweet chocolate
1/4 cup (1/2 stick) butter

Combine 1/2 cup butter, brown sugar, baking cocoa, egg, graham cracker crumbs, coconut and walnuts in a medium bowl and mix well. Press over the bottom of a 9-inch square pan and chill for 30 minutes.

Combine the confectioners' sugar, 1/4 cup butter, cream and custard powder in a medium bowl and beat until smooth and fluffy. Spread carefully over the top of the chilled mixture.

Melt the chocolate and 1/4 cup butter in the top of a double boiler over low heat, stirring until smooth. Spread over the top and chill until firm. Cut into 1-inch squares to serve.

Serves 81 gems

CHOCOLATE TRUFFLES

8 ounces cream cheese, softened
4 cups sifted confectioners' sugar
1 teaspoon ginger
5 ounces unsweetened chocolate, melted, cooled
2 cups semisweet chocolate chips

Beat the cream cheese in a large bowl for 30 seconds or until fluffy. Add the confectioners' sugar and ginger gradually, mixing well after each addition. Add the unsweetened chocolate and beat until well mixed. Spoon into a 9-inch square pan and freeze for 30 minutes or until set.

Shape the mixture into 1-inch balls using a melon baller. Place the balls on a parchment-lined baking sheet and freeze for 15 minutes or until firm.

Melt the chocolate chips in the top of a double boiler over simmering water until completely melted and smooth. Let stand at room temperature to cool until the chocolate begins to set at the edge of the pan.

Drop the truffles into the melted chocolate and remove with a fork or slotted spoon, allowing any excess chocolate to drip back into the pan. Garnish as desired.

Makes 40 truffles

HELPFUL HINT

There are a number of Chocolate Truffle garnishes. You may roll the freshly dipped truffles in a shallow dish of finely ground nuts or chocolate sprinkles, or place on a plate and sift confectioners' sugar or baking cocoa over the top, turning to coat evenly. Alternatively, add 2 tablespoons liqueur of choice, such as amaretto, Cointreau, or framboise to the cream cheese mixture before freezing and shaping, or add 1/2 cup finely chopped toasted nuts, such as pistachios or walnuts. Then roll the chocolate-dipped truffles in finely chopped pistachios or walnuts to garnish.

Frozen Chocolate Peppermint Dessert

1 cup vanilla wafer crumbs
2/3 cup butter or margarine
2 ounces unsweetened chocolate
2 egg yolks
2 cups (or more) confectioners' sugar, sifted
1 teaspoon vanilla extract
2 egg whites
1/2 cup chopped pecans
milk
1/2 gallon peppermint ice cream, softened
1/2 cup vanilla wafer crumbs

Sprinkle 1 cup vanilla wafer crumbs evenly into an ungreased 9×13-inch metal pan. Melt the butter and chocolate in the top of a double boiler over low heat until smooth, stirring frequently. Remove from the heat.

Beat the egg yolks in a large mixing bowl until thick and pale yellow. Add the chocolate mixture, confectioners' sugar and vanilla, beating until smooth.

Beat the egg whites in a bowl until stiff peaks form. Fold into the chocolate mixture gently. Fold in the pecans. Thicken the mixture with additional confectioners' sugar or thin the mixture with milk if necessary for a spreading consistency.

Spoon the chocolate mixture evenly over the wafer crumbs in the pan, smoothing the top to form an even layer. Spread the ice cream evenly over the top and sprinkle with the 1/2 cup vanilla wafer crumbs. Cover with foil and freeze until firm. Cut into 2- to 3-inch squares to serve.

Serves 15 to 18

GODIVA CHOCOLATE CUPS

4 ounces Godiva baking chocolate, chopped
4 egg yolks
1/2 cup confectioners' sugar
1/2 cup heavy cream
4 egg whites

Melt the chocolate in the top of a double boiler over very low heat (110 degrees maximum), stirring until smooth. Remove from the heat. Combine the chocolate with the egg yolks, confectioners' sugar and cream in a blender and blend at low speed for 2 to 3 minutes or until smooth. Add the egg whites and blend for 3 to 4 minutes or until smooth. Pour into 4 demitasse cups or ramekins and chill for 8 hours or longer. Serve garnished with a dollop of sweetened whipped cream flavored with orange liqueur.

Serves 4

PEACH AMARETTO ICE CREAM DESSERT

2 pints vanilla ice cream, softened
3 tablespoons amaretto
2 tablespoons brandy
6 ripe peaches, peeled, sliced
1/4 cup sugar
2 tablespoons amaretto
1 cup crushed amaretti

Combine the ice cream, 3 tablespoons of the amaretto and brandy in a freezer container and mix well. Freeze until firm. Combine the peaches, sugar and 2 tablespoons amaretto in a medium bowl and toss to coat. Spoon into 6 dessert bowls and top with a scoop of the ice cream mixture. Sprinkle with the crushed amaretti.

Amaretti are crisp almond-flavored macaroon-type cookies.

Serves 6

HELPFUL HINT

To easily peel peaches, cover with boiling water and let stand for 30 to 45 seconds. Plunge into a bowl of ice water to halt the cooking process. Using a small paring knife, slit the skin and slip it off. Return each peach to the ice water after peeling.

213

SUMMER FRUIT CREPES WITH RASPBERRY SAUCE

HELPFUL HINT

To prevent crepes from sticking to the pan, add a small amount of melted butter to the batter just before cooking.

CREPES

2 eggs
1 tablespoon sugar
3/4 cup flour

1 1/4 cups half-and-half
1/4 cup orange liqueur
1 tablespoon butter, softened

FRUIT FILLING

12 ounces strawberries
6 ounces raspberries
6 ounces blackberries

2 tablespoons sugar
1/3 cup whipped cream

RASPBERRY SAUCE

2 cups raspberries, puréed
1/4 cup orange liqueur

1 tablespoon sugar

TO PREPARE THE CREPES, whisk the eggs in a medium bowl until frothy. Add the sugar and whisk until well mixed. Add the flour alternately with the half-and-half and liqueur, beating well after each addition. Chill, covered, for 1 hour. Remove from the refrigerator and mix well with a whisk. Brush a 6- or 8-inch nonstick crepe pan or skillet lightly with a small amount of the butter. Heat the pan over medium heat. Pour 3 tablespoons of the crepe batter into the hot pan and quickly swirl to evenly coat the pan. Cook until light brown on the bottom. Turn the crepe and cook the other side just until brown. Remove to a sheet of waxed paper. Repeat the cooking process for the remaining crepe batter, stacking the browned crepes between sheets of waxed paper.

TO PREPARE THE FILLING, chop the strawberries, raspberries and blackberries finely. Combine the berries, sugar and whipped cream in a bowl and mix well.

TO PREPARE THE SAUCE, strain the puréed raspberries through a sieve into a small saucepan. Add the liqueur and sugar and mix well. Warm the mixture over low heat, stirring occasionally.

To serve, spoon 3 tablespoons of the filling down the center of each crepe and roll to enclose the filling. Place 2 filled crepes on each serving plate and top each with a generous tablespoon of the warm sauce.

Serves 7 or 8

LEMON ICE CREAM

1 3/4 cups sugar
2 cups heavy cream
2 cups milk
3/4 teaspoon lemon extract
juice of 4 lemons
grated lemon zest to taste

Combine the sugar, cream, milk, lemon extract, lemon juice and lemon zest in a large bowl and mix well. Pour into an ice cream freezer container and freeze using the manufacturer's directions.

Serves 12

THREE-FRUIT SHERBET

4 cups sugar
5 bananas, mashed
6 cups water
4 cups light cream
juice of 6 oranges
juice of 6 lemons

Combine the sugar, bananas, water, cream, orange juice and lemon juice in a large bowl and mix well. Pour into an ice cream freezer container and freeze using the manufacturer's directions.

Serves 16

HELPFUL HINT

Gingered Fruit makes a quick summer dessert. Just toss 1/2 cup fresh blueberries and 1 small peeled and sliced peach in a bowl. Add 1 teaspoon chopped candied ginger and toss gently. Sprinkle with chopped fresh mint to taste and serve immediately.

Bon Ton Bread Pudding

Bread Pudding

1 loaf French bread, torn into
   1-inch pieces
4 cups milk
3 eggs

2 cups sugar
2 tablespoons vanilla extract
1 cup raisins
3 tablespoons butter, melted

Whiskey Sauce

1/2 cup (1 stick) butter, softened
1 cup sugar

1 egg, beaten
whiskey to taste

To prepare the pudding, combine the bread pieces and milk in a large bowl and let stand to soak. Stir the mixture with a fork to mix well. Beat the eggs, sugar and vanilla in a bowl. Stir in the raisins. Stir the egg mixture into the bread mixture.

Coat the bottom of a 9×13-inch baking pan with the butter. Pour the bread mixture into the prepared pan. Bake at 375 degrees for 40 to 45 minutes or until very firm. Cool on a wire rack.

To prepare the sauce, heat the butter and sugar in the top of a double boiler until the butter is melted and sugar is dissolved, stirring constantly. Beat in the egg quickly. Remove from the heat and allow to cool. Stir in the whiskey.

To serve, cut the cooled pudding into squares and place on individual ovenproof serving dishes. Top each with the sauce and broil until bubbly.

Serves 9 to 12

COLD GINGER SOUFFLÉ

8 egg yolks
2/3 cup sugar
4 cups milk, scalded
3 tablespoons unflavored gelatin
3/4 cup cold water
3/4 cup thinly sliced candied ginger
8 egg whites
1 1/2 cups whipping cream, whipped, chilled

Fold waxed paper or parchment in half and wrap around a
2 1/2-quart soufflé dish to form a collar extending 3 inches above
the edge of the dish; secure in place with kitchen twine.

Beat the egg yolks and sugar in the top of a double boiler. Cook
over simmering water until the mixture is pale yellow and falls
from the spoon in ribbons. Remove from the heat and add the hot
milk in a fine stream, whisking constantly. Return to low heat
over double boiler and stir with a wooden spoon until the custard
coats the spoon. Place the bottom of the double boiler directly
into a bowl of ice water to halt the cooking process.

Sprinkle the gelatin over 3/4 cup water in a medium bowl. Let
stand for 5 minutes to soften. Add to the warm custard and stir
until gelatin is completely dissolved. Add the ginger and stir until
the mixture begins to thicken. Remove from the ice water.

Beat the egg whites in a medium bowl until soft peaks form. Fold
the egg whites and whipped cream gently into the chilled custard.
Pour into the prepared dish and chill for 4 to 6 hours or until
firm. Remove the collar just before serving and garnish with
whipped cream rosettes, finely chopped pistachio nuts or
additional candied ginger slices. You may also use individual
soufflé molds and chill for 2 hours or until firm.

Serves 12

PUMPKIN PRALINE TORTE

1 1/2 cups ground gingersnaps
6 tablespoons (3/4 stick) butter, melted
2 pints pralines and cream ice cream or
  butter pecan ice cream, softened
1 cup chopped pecans

1 (16-ounce) can pumpkin
2 cups sugar
2 1/2 teaspoons cinnamon
2 teaspoons nutmeg
1 1/2 cups whipping cream, whipped

Combine the gingersnaps and butter in a small bowl and mix well. Press over the bottom of a 9-inch springform pan. Bake at 350 degrees for 10 minutes. Cool on a wire rack. Spread the ice cream evenly over the cooled crust and freeze until firm. Sprinkle evenly with the pecans.

Combine the pumpkin, sugar, cinnamon and nutmeg in a medium saucepan and mix well. Bring to a boil over medium-high heat, stirring constantly. Remove from the heat and allow to cool completely. Fold the whipped cream into the cooled pumpkin mixture. Pour into the prepared pan and freeze until firm. Remove to the refrigerator 2 hours before serving time. Loosen and remove the side of the pan to serve.

Serves 8 to 10

BISCUIT TORTONI

2 egg yolks
1/2 cup sugar
salt to taste
2/3 cup milk, scalded

1/2 teaspoon vanilla extract
2 egg whites, stiffly beaten
1 cup almond macaroon crumbs
1 cup whipping cream, whipped

Beat the egg yolks in the top of a double boiler. Cook over simmering water until thick and pale yellow. Add the sugar and salt and mix well. Stir in the milk. Cook until the sugar is dissolved and the mixture is thick, stirring constantly. Cool to room temperature. Stir in the vanilla and fold in the egg whites. Fold in the macaroon crumbs and whipped cream. Spoon into 4 parfait glasses. Chill for 8 hours or longer before serving.

You may top with additional whipped cream, macaroon crumbs and a cherry. May substitute plain macaroons and 1/2 teaspoon almond extract for the almond macaroons.

Serves 4

FRANGELICO FANTASY DESSERT

HAZELNUT ALMOND CRUST
1/2 cup graham cracker crumbs
1/2 cup finely chopped hazelnuts
1 cup finely chopped almonds

1/2 cup sugar
1/2 cup (1 stick) unsalted butter,
    melted

CHOCOLATE LAYER
2 cups heavy cream
16 ounces semisweet chocolate,
    coarsely chopped

2 tablespoons corn syrup
1/2 cup (1 stick) unsalted butter, cut
    into pieces

BUTTERCREAM LAYER
1 1/2 cups sugar
1/2 cup water
6 large egg yolks
1 1/2 cups (3 sticks) unsalted butter,
    softened

1/3 cup Frangelico
4 ounces bittersweet chocolate,
    chopped, melted, cooled

TO PREPARE THE CRUST, combine the graham cracker crumbs, hazelnuts, almonds, sugar and butter in a bowl and mix well. Press over the bottom of a lightly oiled 9 1/2-inch springform pan. Bake at 350 degrees on the middle oven rack for 15 minutes or until light golden brown. Cool on a wire rack.

TO PREPARE THE CHOCOLATE LAYER, combine the cream, chocolate and corn syrup in a saucepan. Cook over medium-high heat until the mixture bubbles and the chocolate melts. Remove from the heat and stir in the butter 1 piece at a time. Spread in the prepared springform pan and chill for 3 hours or until firm.

TO PREPARE THE BUTTERCREAM LAYER, combine the sugar and water in a saucepan. Cook over medium-high heat until the sugar dissolves, stirring occasionally. Simmer until the mixture reaches 240 degrees on a candy thermometer; do not stir.

Beat the egg yolks in a mixing bowl until smooth. Add the hot sugar syrup very gradually, beating constantly at high speed until thickened and cooled. Add the butter gradually, beating at medium speed after each addition. Beat in the Frangelico and chocolate.

Spread the buttercream mixture over the chilled chocolate layer. Chill for 3 hours or until firm. Loosen from the side of the pan with a knife and remove the side of the pan. Place on a serving plate.

Serves 12

AUNT CHICK'S ANGEL FOOD CAKE

$1^1/2$ cups egg whites
$1^1/2$ teaspoons cream of tartar
1 teaspoon salt
$^1/2$ teaspoon almond extract
$^1/2$ teaspoon lemon extract
1 teaspoon vanilla extract
$1^1/2$ cups sugar, sifted
1 cup cake flour, sifted

Beat the egg whites, cream of tartar and salt in a mixing bowl until stiff peaks form. Fold in the almond, lemon and vanilla extracts gently. Fold in the sugar gradually. Fold in the flour gently. Spoon into an ungreased tube pan. Bake at 275 degrees for 15 minutes.

Increase the oven temperature to 300 degrees and bake for 45 minutes longer. Invert on a funnel to cool completely. Loosen the cake from the side of the pan and invert onto a cake plate.

Serves 10 to 12

Nettie McBirney, known as Aunt Chick, started writing a cooking column for the Tulsa Daily World *in 1935. The story goes that her husband, a prominent banker in town, first learned of her journalistic endeavor when he read her column at the breakfast table. He bounded up the stairs looking for her, worried there would be a run on the bank if customers thought his wife had to work.*

She introduced cookie cutters designed for easier dough release in 1948. Today, they are in use throughout the world.

APRICOT CRUMBLE CAKE

CAKE
1/2 cup (1 stick) butter, softened
1 1/4 cups sugar
8 ounces cream cheese, softened
2 eggs
1/4 cup milk

1 teaspoon vanilla extract
2 cups sifted cake flour
1 teaspoon baking powder
1/4 teaspoon salt
1 (12-ounce) jar apricot preserves

COCONUT FROSTING
2 cups shredded coconut
2/3 cup packed brown sugar

1 teaspoon cinnamon
1/3 cup butter, melted

TO PREPARE THE CAKE, cream the butter, sugar and cream cheese in a large bowl until light and fluffy. Add the eggs 1 at a time, mixing well after each addition. Add the milk and vanilla gradually, mixing well. Sift the flour, baking powder and salt together. Add the sifted dry ingredients to the creamed mixture and mix well.

Pour half the batter into a greased and floured 9×13-inch baking pan. Spread the preserves evenly over the batter and spread the remaining batter over the top. Bake at 350 degrees for 35 to 40 minutes or until cake tests done. Cool slightly on a wire rack.

TO PREPARE THE FROSTING, combine the coconut, brown sugar, cinnamon and butter in a medium bowl and mix well. Spread lightly over the top of the warm cake. Broil for 1 to 2 minutes or until golden brown.

Serves 15

Blue Ribbon Frosted Chocolate Cake

Cake

2 1/2 cups sifted flour
1/2 cup sifted baking cocoa
1 cup buttermilk
2 teaspoons baking soda
2 cups sugar

2 eggs
1 cup shortening
1 teaspoon vanilla extract
1 cup boiling water

Chocolate Frosting

1 (1-pound) package confectioners' sugar
1/2 cup (1 stick) butter, softened

8 ounces cream cheese, softened
3 tablespoons baking cocoa

To prepare the cake, whisk the flour and baking cocoa in a small bowl. Combine the buttermilk and baking soda in a small bowl and mix well.

Cream the sugar and eggs in a large mixing bowl until light and fluffy. Add the shortening and vanilla to the creamed mixture and beat until smooth. Add the dry ingredients alternately with the buttermilk mixture, mixing well by hand after each addition. Add the water and mix by hand until well blended.

Spoon the batter evenly into 3 greased and floured 8-inch round cake pans or 1 greased and floured 8×11-inch baking pan. Bake at 350 degrees for 30 to 40 minutes or until a wooden pick inserted in the cake comes out clean. Remove to a wire rack to cool.

To prepare the frosting, cream the confectioners' sugar and butter in a medium mixing bowl. Blend in the cream cheese and baking cocoa, mixing until of spreading consistency.

Spread the frosting between the layers and over the top and side of the cooled cake.

Serves 8

FLOURLESS CHOCOLATE CAKE WITH BERRY SAUCE

CAKE
12 ounces bittersweet chocolate
3/4 cup (1 1/2 sticks) butter,
   cut into pieces
6 egg yolks

6 tablespoons sugar
2 teaspoons vanilla extract
6 egg whites
6 tablespoons sugar

CHOCOLATE CREAM GLAZE
1/3 cup heavy cream
1/3 cup dark corn syrup

6 ounces bittersweet chocolate,
   finely chopped

BERRY SAUCE
3 cups fresh strawberries, hulled
1 1/2 cups fresh raspberries or
   drained thawed frozen raspberries

3/4 cup confectioners' sugar
6 tablespoons Grand Marnier or
   orange liqueur of choice

TO PREPARE THE CAKE, butter a 9-inch springform pan. Line the bottom of the pan with buttered parchment or waxed paper. Wrap the outside of the pan with foil. Melt the chocolate and butter in a heavy medium saucepan over low heat, stirring until smooth. Remove from the heat and cool to lukewarm, stirring frequently. Beat the egg yolks with 6 tablespoons sugar in a large mixing bowl for 3 minutes or until the mixture is very thick and pale yellow. Beat in the vanilla. Add to the chocolate mixture and mix well. Beat the egg whites in a medium bowl until soft peaks form. Add 6 tablespoons sugar gradually, beating until medium-firm peaks form. Fold into the chocolate mixture 1/3 at a time. Spoon the batter into the prepared pan. Bake at 350 degrees for 50 minutes or until the top is puffed and cracked and a cake tester inserted in the center comes out with moist crumbs attached. Cool in the pan on a wire rack. Press the top down to even the thickness of the cake. Loosen the cake from the side of the pan with a small knife. Remove the side of the pan and place a round cake board over the top; invert the cake. Peel off the parchment paper.

TO PREPARE THE GLAZE, combine the cream and corn syrup in a medium saucepan and mix well. Bring the mixture to a simmer over low heat. Remove from the heat and stir in the chocolate, whisking until melted and smooth.

TO PREPARE THE SAUCE, combine the strawberries and raspberries in a food processor and purée until smooth. Add the confectioners' sugar and Grand Marnier and process until well blended. Strain the sauce through a sieve to remove any seeds.

To assemble, place the cake on a wire rack set over a baking sheet. Spread 1/2 cup of the glaze over the top and side of the cake. Freeze for 3 minutes or until almost set. Pour the remaining glaze over the cake, allowing the excess to drip onto the baking sheet. Chill for 1 hour or until the glaze is firm. Serve at room temperature with the sauce.

Serves 10 to 12

GLAZED POUND CAKE

HELPFUL HINT

To easily fill a tube pan, cover the hole with a paper cup.

CAKE
1 cup (2 sticks) butter, softened
1/2 cup shortening
3 cups sugar
3 cups flour
1 teaspoon baking powder
salt to taste
1 cup milk
5 eggs
1 teaspoon coconut flavoring
1 teaspoon rum flavoring
1 teaspoon butter flavoring

FOUR-FLAVOR GLAZE
1 cup sugar
1/2 cup water
1 teaspoon coconut flavoring
1 teaspoon rum flavoring
1 teaspoon butter flavoring
1 teaspoon almond flavoring

TO PREPARE THE CAKE, cream the butter, shortening and sugar in a large mixing bowl until light and fluffy. Sift the flour, baking powder and salt together. Add the sifted dry ingredients to the creamed mixture alternately with the milk, mixing well after each addition. Beat in the eggs and flavorings.

Spoon into a greased and floured bundt pan. Bake at 325 degrees for 1 1/2 hours or until the cake tests done. Remove to a wire rack.

TO PREPARE THE GLAZE, combine the sugar, water and flavorings in a small saucepan and mix well. Heat over medium-low heat until the sugar is dissolved and mixture is heated through; do not boil. Pour over the warm cake and let stand until cool.

The flavor improves if allowed to stand for several days before serving.

Serves 16

TOASTED SPICE CAKE

3/4 cup (1 1/2 sticks) butter, softened
2 cups packed brown sugar
2 egg yolks, beaten
2 1/3 cups cake flour
1 teaspoon baking powder
1 teaspoon baking soda
3/4 teaspoon salt
1 teaspoon cinnamon
1/2 teaspoon ground cloves
1 1/4 cups buttermilk
1 teaspoon vanilla extract
1 cup packed brown sugar
2 egg whites, stiffly beaten
nuts to taste

Cream the butter and 2 cups brown sugar in a large bowl until light and fluffy. Beat in the egg yolks. Sift the flour, baking powder, baking soda, salt, cinnamon and cloves together three times. Add the sifted dry ingredients to the creamed mixture alternately with the buttermilk, mixing well after each addition. Stir in the vanilla. Spoon into a greased 9×13-inch cake pan.

Add 1 cup brown sugar gradually to the stiffly beaten egg whites, mixing until smooth. Spread over the cake batter, sealing to the edges of the pan. Sprinkle evenly with nuts. Bake at 350 degrees for 30 minutes or until the cake tests done.

Serves 15

Princess White Cake with Pineapple and Lemon Filling

Cake

2 cups minus 2 tablespoons sifted
  flour
1 1/4 cups sugar
3 1/2 teaspoons baking powder
1 teaspoon salt
1 cup minus 2 tablespoons milk

1 teaspoon vanilla extract
3/4 teaspoon almond extract
1/4 teaspoon orange extract
1/2 cup shortening
3 egg whites

Pineapple and Lemon Filling

3/4 cup sugar
2 1/2 tablespoons cornstarch
1/8 teaspoon salt
grated zest of 1 lemon
1/4 cup lemon juice

1/2 cup pineapple juice
3 egg yolks, beaten
2 tablespoons butter, softened
2 cups (or more) whipping cream,
  whipped

To prepare the cake, sift the flour, sugar, baking powder and salt into a mixing bowl. Add the milk, flavorings and shortening and beat for 2 minutes or until well blended. Add the egg whites and beat for 2 minutes. Spread the batter in 2 greased and floured round 8-inch cake pans. Bake at 350 degrees for 25 to 30 minutes or until cake tests done. Cool in the pans for 10 to 15 minutes. Remove to a wire rack to cool completely.

To prepare the filling, combine the sugar, cornstarch and salt in the top of a double boiler and mix well. Stir in the lemon zest and lemon juice. Add the pineapple juice, egg yolks and butter and mix well. Cook over boiling water until smooth and thickened, stirring constantly. Cool to room temperature.

To assemble, slice each cake layer into halves horizontally. Place 1 of the 4 cake layers on a cake plate and spread evenly with one-third of the pineapple and lemon mixture and a thin layer of the whipped cream. Place the second cake layer on top and spread with half the remaining pineapple and lemon mixture and a thin layer of the whipped cream. Top with the third cake layer and spread with the remaining pineapple and lemon mixture and a thin layer of the whipped cream. Top with the remaining cake layer and frost the top and side of the entire cake with the remaining whipped cream. Chill until serving time. Cut into thin slices to serve.

Serves 12

TUXEDO BROWNIE SQUARES

BROWNIES
1 cup (2 sticks) butter
3 tablespoons baking cocoa
2 cups sugar
1 1/2 cups flour
4 eggs, beaten
1 teaspoon vanilla extract

RASPBERRY AND WHITE CHOCOLATE TOPPING
16 ounces cream cheese, softened
1/2 cup confectioners' sugar
3 ounces white chocolate, melted, slightly cooled
1/4 cup milk
8 ounces whipped topping
1/2 cup seedless raspberry jam
2 cups fresh raspberries, or frozen whole unsweetened raspberries, thawed, drained

TO PREPARE THE BROWNIES, melt the butter in a large saucepan over low heat. Add the baking cocoa and mix well. Add the sugar, flour, eggs and vanilla and mix well. Spread in a greased and floured 9×13-inch baking pan. Bake at 350 degrees for 40 minutes or until the brownies pull away from the sides of the pan. Cool on a wire rack.

TO PREPARE THE TOPPING, cream the cream cheese and confectioners' sugar in a medium bowl until light and fluffy. Whisk in the melted chocolate and milk gradually until well blended. Fold in the whipped topping.

Spread the jam evenly over the cooled brownies and top with 1 1/2 cups of the raspberries. Spread the white chocolate mixture carefully over the raspberries and chill for 1 hour or until firm. Top with the remaining 1/2 cup raspberries and garnish with Chocolate Leaves (at right) or chocolate curls. Store, covered, in the refrigerator.

Serves 10 to 12

HELPFUL HINT

To make Chocolate Leaves, choose nonpoisonous leaves, such as camellia, ficus, rose, lemon or lime, that have not been treated with pesticides. Wipe the leaves well. Melt semisweet chocolate in the top of a double boiler over hot, not boiling, water. Brush the chocolate in a thick layer over the veined underside of the leaves. Freeze the coated leaves and gently peel the wilted leaves from the hardened chocolate. Use the chocolate leaves to decorate as desired. Store any leftover chocolate leaves on waxed paper in the refrigerator.

CEREAL KILLERS

HELPFUL HINT

To avoid adding more liquid to crumbly cookie dough, cover the dough with a slightly damp cloth and let stand at room temperature for 30 minutes.

1 cup (2 sticks) butter, softened
1 cup sugar
1 1/2 cups flour
1 teaspoon baking soda
1 teaspoon cream of tartar
1 1/2 teaspoons vanilla extract
2 cups crisp rice cereal
1/2 cup chopped nuts

Cream the butter and sugar in a mixing bowl until light and fluffy. Sift the flour, baking soda and cream of tartar together. Add the sifted dry ingredients to the creamed mixture and mix until smooth. Blend in the vanilla. Stir in the cereal and nuts.

Shape the mixture into balls and arrange on an ungreased cookie sheet, leaving space for the cookies to spread. Flatten the balls into 1/4-inch thickness. Bake at 350 degrees for 12 minutes or until light brown. Cool on a wire rack. Remove and store in an airtight container.

You may prepare the dough in advance and chill until ready to bake. Remove from the refrigerator and bring almost to room temperature before proceeding.

Makes 3 to 4 dozen   *Photograph for this recipe appears on page 206.*

CARAMEL COOKIE CUPS

COOKIE CUPS
1 cup (2 sticks) margarine, softened
8 ounces cream cheese, softened
2 cups flour
1 (14-ounce) package caramels
1/2 cup evaporated milk

VANILLA FROSTING
1/2 cup shortening
1/2 cup (1 stick) margarine, softened
2/3 cup sugar
3/4 cup evaporated milk
1 teaspoon vanilla extract
1 cup walnuts, finely chopped

TO PREPARE THE COOKIE CUPS, cream the margarine and cream cheese in a mixing bowl until light and fluffy. Add the flour and mix until smooth. Shape the dough into 1-inch balls and press over the bottoms and up the sides of 40 to 45 greased miniature muffin cups. Bake at 350 degrees for 15 to 20 minutes or until light brown. Remove from pans and arrange the cups on a cookie sheet.

Melt the caramels with the evaporated milk in the top of a double boiler over simmering water, stirring until smooth and creamy. Spoon into the cookie cups. Cool to room temperature.

TO PREPARE THE FROSTING, cream the shortening, margarine and sugar in a medium mixing bowl until light and fluffy. Add the evaporated milk and vanilla and beat until smooth and fluffy. Spread over the filled cookie cups or pipe over the top using a pastry bag fitted with a decorating tip. Sprinkle with the walnuts.

Makes 40 to 45

CHOCOLATE COCONUT PUFFS

2 egg whites
1/2 cup sugar
1/4 teaspoon salt
1/2 teaspoon vanilla extract
1 cup chocolate chips, melted
1/2 cup flaked coconut

Beat the egg whites in a bowl until foamy. Add the sugar gradually, beating until stiff peaks form. Beat in the salt and vanilla. Fold in the chocolate and coconut. Drop the dough by spoonfuls onto a parchment-lined cookie sheet. Bake at 325 degrees for 20 minutes. Cool slightly on the cookie sheet. Remove to a wire rack to cool completely. Store in an airtight container.

Makes 1 dozen

SOUTHERN HILLS ALMOND MACAROONS

14 ounces almond paste
1 cup sugar
1 cup confectioners' sugar
1/4 cup cornmeal
2 tablespoons honey
4 egg whites

Combine the almond paste, sugar, confectioners' sugar, cornmeal, honey and egg whites in a bowl and mix until smooth. Pipe onto a parchment-lined cookie sheet using a pastry bag fitted with the desired tip. Pat the cookie tops lightly with a damp towel. Bake at 350 degrees for 8 to 10 minutes or until light brown. Serve immediately.

Thanks to Chef Devin of the Southern Hills Country Club for sharing this popular cookie recipe.

Makes 2 dozen

COCONUT AND OATMEAL COOKIES

2 cups rolled oats
2 cups flaked coconut
1/2 cup nuts
2 cups flour, sifted
1 teaspoon baking powder
1/2 cup (1 stick) butter, softened
1/2 cup shortening
1 cup sugar
1 cup packed brown sugar
2 eggs, beaten
2 teaspoons vanilla extract

Combine the oats, coconut and nuts in a food processor and process until finely ground. Sift the flour and baking powder together. Cream the butter, shortening, sugar and brown sugar in a large mixing bowl until light and fluffy. Add the eggs and vanilla and beat until smooth. Add the sifted dry ingredients and mix well. Stir in the ground coconut mixture.

Shape the dough into balls and place on a greased cookie sheet. Press each dough ball 1/2 inch thick with the tines of a fork. Top each cookie with a maraschino cherry or nut half. Bake at 350 degrees for 30 minutes or until brown. Cool on a wire rack.

Makes 6 to 7 dozen

COOKIE JAR GINGERSNAPS

3/4 cup shortening
1 cup sugar
1 egg
1/4 cup molasses
1 teaspoon vanilla extract
2 cups flour
1 tablespoon ground ginger
2 teaspoons baking soda
1 teaspoon cinnamon
1/2 teaspoon salt
sugar for coating

Cream the shortening and 1 cup sugar in a medium mixing bowl until light and fluffy. Add the egg, molasses and vanilla and mix well. Sift the flour, ginger, baking soda, cinnamon and salt together. Add the sifted dry ingredients to the creamed mixture and mix well.

Shape the dough into 1-inch balls and roll in additional sugar to coat. Arrange 2 inches apart on a nonstick cookie sheet. Bake at 350 degrees for 10 to 12 minutes or until brown. The longer baking time makes for a crisper cookie, so adjust the time to suit individual tastes.

Makes 3 to 4 dozen

Peanut Butterscotch Cookies

$1/2$ cup (1 stick) butter, softened
$1/2$ cup chunky peanut butter
$1/2$ cup sugar
$3/4$ cup packed brown sugar
1 egg
1 teaspoon vanilla extract
$2/3$ cup quick-cooking oats
$3/4$ cup chopped dry-roasted peanuts
$1 1/2$ cups butterscotch chips
$1 1/4$ cups flour
$3/4$ teaspoon baking powder
sugar for coating

Cream the butter, peanut butter, sugar and brown sugar in a large mixing bowl until light and fluffy. Add the egg and vanilla and beat until well mixed. Stir in the oats, peanuts and butterscotch chips. Sift the flour and baking powder together. Add to the creamed mixture gradually, mixing well. Chill, covered, for 30 minutes.

Shape by rounded teaspoonfuls into balls and arrange 2 inches apart on an ungreased cookie sheet. Grease the bottom of a drinking glass and dip in additional sugar. Press each dough ball with the sugared glass to flatten and coat with sugar, recoating the glass with sugar frequently. Bake at 375 degrees for 10 to 12 minutes or until light brown. Cool on the cookie sheet for 1 to 2 minutes. Remove to a wire rack to cool completely.

Makes 2 dozen

SPECIAL SANDIES

1 cup (2 sticks) butter, softened
1 cup vegetable oil
1 cup sugar
1 cup packed brown sugar
1 egg
1 teaspoon vanilla extract
3 1/2 cups flour
1 teaspoon baking soda
1 teaspoon salt
1 cup instant oats
1 cup flaked coconut
1 cup crisp rice cereal
1 cup chopped pecans
sugar for coating

Combine the butter and vegetable oil in a large mixing bowl and beat until smooth. Add the sugar, brown sugar, egg and vanilla and mix well. Sift the flour, baking soda and salt together. Add to the creamed mixture and mix well. Stir in the oats, coconut, cereal and pecans.

Drop by rounded tablespoonfuls 2 inches apart onto a nonstick cookie sheet. Press each dough portion with the flat bottom of a drinking glass dipped in additional sugar to flatten slightly. Bake at 350 degrees for 8 to 12 minutes or until light brown. Cool on a wire rack.

Makes 4 to 5 dozen

SUGAR COOKIES

COOKIES

1 cup (2 sticks) butter,
  softened
1 cup sugar
1 cup confectioners' sugar
1 cup vegetable oil
2 eggs

1 tablespoon vanilla extract
4 1/2 cups flour
1 teaspoon salt
1 teaspoon baking soda
1 teaspoon cream of tartar
sugar for coating

BUTTER AND CREAM CHEESE FROSTING

1/2 cup (1 stick) butter,
  softened
3 ounces cream cheese,
  softened
1 (1-pound) package
  confectioners' sugar, sifted

1 teaspoon (or more) vanilla
  extract
food coloring

TO PREPARE THE COOKIES, cream the butter, 1 cup sugar and confectioners' sugar in a large mixing bowl until light and fluffy. Add the vegetable oil, eggs and vanilla and beat until smooth. Sift the flour, salt, baking soda and cream of tartar together. Add to the creamed mixture and mix well. Chill, covered, in the refrigerator. Shape the dough into balls and place 2 inches apart on an ungreased cookie sheet. Press the dough balls to flatten with the flat bottom of a drinking glass dipped in additional sugar, redipping the glass in sugar before pressing each ball. Bake at 350 degrees for 10 to 12 minutes or until light brown. Cool on a wire rack.

TO PREPARE THE FROSTING, cream the butter and cream cheese in a medium bowl until light and fluffy. Add the confectioners' sugar and vanilla and beat until smooth and of spreading consistency. Tint as desired with food coloring. Spread over the cookies and decorate as desired with red hot cinnamon candies, raisins or other toppings.

You may substitute a mixture of vanilla, almond and/or lemon extracts for the vanilla in the frosting. You may use liquid, powdered or paste food coloring in the frosting. Powdered or paste food coloring is more intense than liquid.

Makes 6 dozen

HELPFUL HINT

To make Cookie Paint for decorating cookies, combine 1 large egg yolk with 1/4 teaspoon water in a small bowl for each color desired and mix well. Stir in enough liquid food coloring to achieve the desired depth of color. Add more water if using powdered or paste food coloring. Place unbaked sugar cookies on parchment-lined cookie sheets. Paint the cookies as desired with the egg yolk paints, using small paint brushes of various widths. Sprinkle with colored sugars or edible glitter before baking as directed. You may also paint baked cookies and return them to the oven briefly to allow the paint to set, watching carefully. Decorated cookies may be wrapped and frozen.

TURTLE COOKIES

2 ounces semisweet chocolate
1/3 cup butter or margarine
2 eggs, beaten
3/4 cup sugar
1 teaspoon vanilla extract
1 cup flour
frosting of choice

Melt the chocolate and butter in a heavy saucepan over low heat, stirring until smooth; cool. Combine the eggs, sugar, vanilla and cooled chocolate mixture in a large mixing bowl and mix well. Add the flour and mix well.

Spray a waffle iron with nonstick cooking spray and preheat to medium. Spoon the batter by teaspoonfuls 2 inches apart onto the hot waffle iron. Cook for 1 to 1 1/2 minutes or until the cookies are cooked through. Cool on a wire rack and frost as desired and garnish with pecan halves.

Makes 2 dozen

VIRGIN ISLAND CHEWY COOKIES

1 cup (2 sticks) butter, softened
2 cups flour
1 cup packed light brown sugar
4 eggs, lightly beaten
1/2 teaspoon vanilla extract
1/4 cup flour
1 teaspoon salt
3 cups packed dark brown sugar
1 cup flaked coconut
2 cups pecans, coarsely chopped
1/4 cup confectioners' sugar

Combine the butter, 2 cups flour and light brown sugar in a large mixing bowl and beat until smooth. Spread over the bottom of a nonstick 9×13-inch baking pan. Bake at 350 degrees for 15 minutes. Cool on a wire rack. Reduce oven temperature to 325 degrees.

Combine the eggs, vanilla, 1/4 cup flour, salt and dark brown sugar in a large bowl and mix well. Stir in the coconut and pecans and spread over the baked layer. Bake at 325 degrees for 35 to 40 minutes or until firm. Sift the confectioners' sugar evenly over the top. Cool and cut into small squares to serve.

Makes 48 squares

APPLE TART

TART PASTRY
1/2 cup (1 stick) butter, softened
1/2 cup sugar
1 1/4 cups flour

APPLE FILLING
3 Granny Smith apples, peeled, cored, sliced
1/2 cup packed brown sugar
1/4 teaspoon cinnamon
1/4 teaspoon nutmeg
1/4 teaspoon allspice
8 ounces cream cheese, softened
1/2 cup sugar
2 cups half-and-half
1 teaspoon vanilla extract
3 eggs
1 egg yolk

TO PREPARE THE PASTRY, cream the butter and sugar in a medium mixing bowl until light and fluffy. Add the flour and mix to form a dough. Press over the bottom and up the side of an 11-inch tart pan. Chill for 1 hour.

TO PREPARE THE FILLING, combine the apples, brown sugar, cinnamon, nutmeg and allspice in a large saucepan and toss to coat. Heat over medium-high heat until the sugar is dissolved, stirring constantly. Pour into the chilled tart shell.

Combine the cream cheese, sugar, half-and-half, vanilla, eggs and egg yolk in a large bowl and beat until well blended. Pour over the apple mixture. Bake at 350 degrees for 1 hour or until the top is golden brown. Serve warm or at room temperature.

Serves 8

Apple Buttermilk Custard Pie

Pie

1/2 (15-ounce) package refrigerated
   pie crusts
1/4 cup (1/2 stick) butter
2 Granny Smith apples, peeled,
   sliced
1/2 cup sugar
1/2 teaspoon cinnamon

1/4 cup (1/2 stick) butter, softened
1 1/3 cups sugar
4 eggs
2 tablespoons flour
1 teaspoon vanilla extract
3/4 cup buttermilk

Brown Sugar Topping

3 tablespoons butter
1/4 cup sugar
1/4 cup packed light brown sugar

1/2 cup flour
1/4 teaspoon cinnamon

To prepare the pie, fit the pastry into a 9-inch pie plate; trim the edge and prick bottom and side with a fork. Melt 1/4 cup butter in a skillet over medium heat. Add the apples, 1/2 cup sugar and cinnamon and toss to coat. Cook for 3 to 5 minutes or until the apples are tender, stirring frequently. Cool slightly. Spoon into the pie shell.

Cream 1/4 cup butter and 1 1/3 cups sugar in a mixing bowl until light and fluffy. Add the eggs 1 at a time, beating just until mixed after each addition. Add the flour and vanilla and beat until well blended. Add the buttermilk and beat until smooth. Spoon over the apples. Bake at 300 degrees for 30 minutes.

To prepare the topping, combine the butter, sugar, brown sugar, flour and cinnamon in a bowl and mix until crumbly. Sprinkle evenly over the partially baked pie. Bake at 300 degrees for 40 minutes longer.

Serves 8

Black Gold Pie

Chocolate Pecan Crust
2 cups chocolate wafer crumbs
3/4 cup chopped pecans

1/2 cup (1 stick) butter, melted

Filling
22 caramels (about 1 cup)
1/4 cup whipping cream
2 tablespoons butter
1 envelope unflavored gelatin
1/4 cup cold water
1 cup whipping cream

1 cup semisweet chocolate chips
1/2 cup whipping cream
2 eggs
1 teaspoon vanilla extract
1/4 cup whipping cream

TO PREPARE THE CRUST, combine the chocolate wafer crumbs, pecans and butter in a medium bowl and mix well. Press over the bottom and up the side of a 9-inch pie plate. Bake at 350 degrees for 10 minutes. Cool on a wire rack.

TO PREPARE THE FILLING, combine the caramels, 1/4 cup cream and butter in a small saucepan and simmer until the butter and caramels are melted and the mixture is smooth, stirring occasionally. Pour into the cooled pie crust and let stand for 10 minutes.

Sprinkle the gelatin over the water in a small saucepan and let stand for 1 minute to soften. Heat over low heat until the gelatin is completely dissolved, stirring constantly. Stir in 1 cup cream and heat just to the boiling point.

Combine the gelatin mixture and chocolate chips in a blender and process until the chocolate is melted. Add 1/2 cup cream, eggs and vanilla, processing constantly until smooth. Pour into a bowl and chill for 15 minutes or until thickened.

Whisk or beat the chilled chocolate mixture until smooth and creamy. Pour over the caramel layer and chill until serving time. Whip 1/4 cup cream in a mixing bowl until soft peaks form. Serve the pie with a dollop of whipped cream.

Serves 8

CLEORA BUTLER'S FUDGE PIE

1^{1}/2 cups heavy cream
1 teaspoon vanilla extract
1^{1}/2 cups sugar
3 tablespoons (heaping) baking cocoa
2 tablespoons (heaping) flour
^{1}/4 teaspoon salt
1 unbaked (9-inch) pie shell, chilled
^{1}/3 cup pecans, chopped

Combine the cream, vanilla and sugar in a medium bowl and mix well. Sift the baking cocoa, flour and salt together 3 times. Add to the cream mixture and mix well. Spoon into the chilled pie shell and sprinkle evenly with the pecans.

Bake at 375 to 400 degrees for 10 minutes. Reduce the oven temperature to 350 degrees and bake for 25 to 30 minutes longer or until set. Serve with a dollop of whipped cream or a scoop of vanilla ice cream.

Serves 6

CHERRY PICKER CREAM PIE

TOASTED ALMOND CRUST
1 cup flour
1/2 teaspoon salt
1/4 cup toasted almonds, chopped
1/3 cup shortening
2 tablespoons cold water

FILLING
1 (14-ounce) can sweetened condensed milk
1/2 cup lemon juice
1 teaspoon vanilla extract
1/2 teaspoon almond extract
1 cup whipping cream, whipped

CHERRY GLAZE
1 (15-ounce) can pitted sour cherries
1/4 cup sugar
1 tablespoon cornstarch
2 or 3 drops red food coloring

TO PREPARE THE CRUST, combine the flour, salt and almonds in a medium bowl and mix well. Cut in the shortening until crumbly. Add the water 1 tablespoon at a time, mixing until the mixture forms a ball. Chill, covered in plastic wrap, for 2 hours or longer. Roll the pastry to fit a 9-inch pie plate; fit into the pie plate and flute the edge. Bake at 350 degrees for 20 minutes or until light brown. Cool on a wire rack.

TO PREPARE THE FILLING, combine the sweetened condensed milk, lemon juice, vanilla and almond extract in a medium mixing bowl and beat until smooth and thickened. Fold in the whipped cream. Pour into the cooled pie crust and chill in the refrigerator.

TO PREPARE THE GLAZE, drain the cherries, reserving 2/3 cup liquid. Combine the reserved cherry liquid, sugar, cornstarch and food coloring in a large saucepan. Cook over medium heat until thick and clear, stirring constantly. Remove from heat and add the cherries, mixing gently. Spread over the chilled filling and chill, covered, for 4 hours or longer.

Serves 8

CRANBERRY PEACH PIE

1 (2-crust) pie pastry
2 cups fresh or frozen cranberries
1/2 cup plus 3 tablespoons sugar
2 tablespoons cornstarch
1 (21-ounce) can peach pie filling
1/8 teaspoon cinnamon
2 drops almond extract
1 egg yolk, beaten
1 teaspoon water

Fit 1 pie pastry into a 9-inch pie plate. Combine the cranberries, sugar and cornstarch in a large bowl and mix well. Add the pie filling, cinnamon and almond extract and mix gently. Spoon into the pie shell. Place the remaining pastry over the top, sealing the edge and cutting vents.

Combine the egg yolk and water in a small bowl and whisk until well blended. Brush evenly over the top of the pastry. Bake at 425 degrees for 30 to 40 minutes or until the crust is golden brown and the filling is bubbly; cover the edge of the pie crust with foil after 15 minutes of baking, if necessary, to prevent overbrowning.

Serves 8

CREAM CHEESE PEANUT BUTTER PIE

COOKIE CRUST
1 cup vanilla wafer crumbs
1/2 cup finely chopped pecans
6 tablespoons (3/4 stick) unsalted butter, melted
2 tablespoons sugar
1/4 teaspoon cinnamon

FILLING
1 1/4 cups creamy peanut butter (no substitutions)
8 ounces cream cheese, softened
1/2 cup confectioners' sugar
2 tablespoons unsalted butter, melted
1 1/4 cups whipping cream, chilled
1/2 cup confectioners' sugar
1 tablespoon vanilla extract

CHOCOLATE GLAZE
1/2 cup heavy cream
4 ounces semisweet chocolate, finely chopped

TO PREPARE THE CRUST, combine the vanilla wafer crumbs, pecans, butter, sugar and cinnamon in a medium bowl and mix well. Press the mixture firmly over the bottom and up the side of a 9-inch pie plate. Freeze until ready to fill.

TO PREPARE THE FILLING, combine the peanut butter, cream cheese, 1/2 cup confectioners' sugar and butter in a large mixing bowl and beat until smooth and creamy. Whip the cream with 1/2 cup confectioners' sugar and vanilla in a medium bowl until soft peaks form. Stir one-fourth of the whipped cream mixture into the peanut butter mixture. Fold in the remaining whipped cream mixture. Spoon into the crust and chill until firm.

TO PREPARE THE GLAZE, bring the cream to a boil in a saucepan over medium heat. Reduce the heat to low and add the chocolate, stirring until melted and smooth. Allow the glaze to cool slightly. Pour over the filling, tipping the pie plate to distribute the glaze evenly. Chill for 1 hour or longer before serving.

You may substitute chocolate wafer crumbs for the vanilla wafer crumbs if desired, and omit the cinnamon. The pie can be prepared 1 day in advance.

Serves 6 to 8

BUTTERMILK PECAN PIE

1/2 cup (1 stick) butter, softened
2 cups sugar
2 1/4 teaspoons vanilla extract
3 eggs
3 tablespoons flour
1/4 teaspoon salt
1 cup buttermilk
1 cup pecan halves
1 unbaked (9-inch) pie shell

Cream the butter and sugar in a mixing bowl until light and fluffy, adding the sugar gradually. Blend in the vanilla. Add the eggs 1 at a time, beating well after each addition. Sift the flour and salt together and add to the creamed mixture gradually, mixing well after each addition. Add the buttermilk and mix well.

Sprinkle the pecans over the bottom of the pie shell, reserving several for the top of the pie. Pour the batter into the pie shell and top with the reserved pecans. Bake at 300 degrees for 1 1/2 hours or until set. Cool on a wire rack. Serve at room temperature.

Serves 6 to 8

LEMON PECAN TART

HELPFUL HINT

For Candied Lemon Zest, bring a small saucepan of water to a boil over medium-high heat. Dip thinly sliced lemon zest into the boiling water 3 times with a slotted spoon. Remove and pat dry with paper towels. Combine 4 parts sugar with 1 part water in a medium saucepan and mix well. Heat to 230 degrees on a candy thermometer, spun-thread stage. Remove from the heat and add the lemon zest, stirring to coat well. Remove the zest to a sugar-lined plate and roll in the sugar to coat completely; cool.

BUTTER CRUST

1 3/4 cups (3 1/2 sticks) butter, softened
2/3 cup superfine sugar

1 1/2 teaspoons vanilla extract
2 2/3 cups flour

FILLING

3 eggs, lightly beaten
1 teaspoon lemon extract
juice of 1 lemon
1 1/2 cups sugar

2 tablespoons butter, melted, cooled
1 1/2 to 2 cups chopped pecans

LEMON CREAM

1 cup sour cream
1 (14-ounce) can sweetened condensed milk

grated zest of 1 lemon
juice of 1 lemon
Candied Lemon Zest (at left)

TO PREPARE THE CRUST, cream the butter and sugar in a large mixing bowl until light and fluffy. Add the vanilla and mix well. Add the flour gradually, mixing well after each addition; mixture will be the consistency of shortbread. Shape into a ball and chill, wrapped in plastic wrap, for 30 minutes. Roll into a 1/4-inch-thick circle on a floured surface and fit into a 10 1/2- to 11-inch buttered and floured tart pan, trimming and fluting the edge.

TO PREPARE THE FILLING, combine the eggs, lemon extract and lemon juice in a medium mixing bowl and beat until light and pale yellow. Combine the sugar and butter in a medium bowl and mix well. Add to the lemon mixture and stir until well blended. Stir in the pecans. Spoon the filling into the prepared pie shell. Bake at 300 degrees for 35 minutes or until crust is golden brown and filling is just set. Cool on a wire rack.

TO PREPARE THE CREAM, combine the sour cream, sweetened condensed milk, lemon zest and lemon juice in a medium bowl and mix well. Chill until serving time.

To serve, drizzle the lemon cream onto a serving plate and top with 1 slice of the tart. Drizzle the tart slice with additional lemon cream and top with Candied Lemon Zest if desired.

Serves 8

LIME LUSH TART

CINNAMON GRAHAM TART SHELL
1 2/3 cups fine graham cracker crumbs
1/4 cup sugar
1/4 teaspoon cinnamon
1/8 teaspoon nutmeg
5 tablespoons butter, melted

FILLING
3 egg yolks, lightly beaten
1 cup sugar
1/3 cup cornstarch
3/4 cup milk
1/2 cup fresh lime juice or lemon juice
1/4 cup (1/2 stick) butter, softened
1 cup sour cream
1 to 2 drops green or yellow food coloring (optional)

TOPPING
1 cup whipping cream
2 to 3 tablespoons confectioners' sugar (optional)

TO PREPARE THE TART SHELL, combine the graham cracker crumbs, sugar, cinnamon, nutmeg and butter in a medium bowl and mix well. Press over the bottom and up the side of a 9-inch tart pan. Bake at 375 degrees for 8 minutes. Cool on a wire rack.

TO PREPARE THE FILLING, combine the egg yolks, sugar, cornstarch and milk in a medium saucepan and mix well. Cook over medium heat for 5 to 7 minutes or until thickened, stirring constantly. Stir in the lime juice. Fold in the butter 1 tablespoon at a time until melted and smooth. Allow the mixture to cool and thicken. Fold in the sour cream and stir in the food coloring. Pour the filling into the cooled crust and chill until ready to serve.

TO PREPARE THE TOPPING, whip the cream and confectioners' sugar in a bowl and spread over the top of the tart. Garnish with grated lime or lemon zest.

Serves 6 to 8

CONTRIBUTORS

SPECIAL THANKS TO OUR GENEROUS SPONSORS

WILDCATTER:

The Bama Companies, Inc.
Stephanie H. Darnell and
    William C. Jackson
Margee McGinnis Filstrup
Helmerich and Payne, Inc.

Terry F. Rigdon, D.D.S.
Katherine Sinclair
Mollie Williford
Wood Oil Company

ROUGHNECK:

Rob and Lisa Berry
T. W. and Shelly Drullinger
Catherine and Tom Fee
Joseph F. Glass
Lee Hanks
Casie Lewis
Dr. Brenda Lloyd-Jones
Roxanna and Robert Lorton
Linda and Bill Loughridge

Sondra Martin
Michelle O'Donnell and Mike Royal
Randy and Mardeen Olmstead
Bobbye Potter
Valerie V. Randolph
Kim Smith
Stanley Funeral Service
Kathleen M. Williams
Conner and Winters

RECIPE CONTRIBUTORS

Louise Allis
Becky Anderson
Lili Anderson
Patricia Knapp Armstrong
Kim Ashley
Jan Auffenberg
Gae Spivey Bachle
Deborah Ball
Terri Banasik
Francine Bandy
Sharon Barnes
Billie Barnett
Lee Anne Barranco
Francey Bates
Debbie Bayouth
Anita Beard
Paula Beasley
Lynne Beason
Sandra Behm
Marjorie Berry
Nancy Bizjack
Sarah Jane McKinney Blevins
Kim Bourke
Elisa Bowen
Mrs. W. W. Bowers
Mary J. Brett
Linda Broach
Debbie Brown
Jadenna Brown

Mandy Brueck
Mary Jane Brueck
Donna Paulus Burch
Jayme Burton
JoAnna M. Burton
Judy Burton
Carol Bush
Leslie Butler
Sharon Smith Butler
Judyth Campbell
Robyn Cannon
Liz Carson
Michelle Carter
Stephanie Cipolla
Revelle Clausing
Debbie Coleman
Debbie Collins
Heather Conklin
Maryde Connor
Barbara Coon
Stephanie Coon
Gail Coskey
Julie Craig
Caroline Owens Crain
Ginny Creveling
The Honorable Thomas S. Crewson
Katherine Croze
Mary Culver
Danae Cupples

Mary Danz
Anne Darnell
Stephanie Darnell
Annette Owen Davis
Lisa DeJarnette
Paula Dellavedova
Karen Dennis
De'Ette Doerr
Denny Doherty
Virgina DonCarlos
Lori Doran
Connie Hamerick Doverspike
Kay Drake
Kelly Dudney
Carey J. Dunkin
Jeannette Dashiell Dunn
Mendi Dunn
Lea Dutton
Sandra Enfinger
Kari Ernest
Laurie Fiocchi
Sue Flynn
Janace Fogleman
Lee Fowler
Paula Fox
Karen Fraser
Leslie Frazier
Judy Freese
Laurie Fuller

Leigh Ann Fuller
Sadie Fuller
Melissa Futrell
D'Ann Gaines
Lu Anna Galles
Stephanie E. Galles
Delia Shelly Garcia
Earlene Walls Gathright
Leigh Gathright
Carla Gilbert
Debbie Gladd
Tiffany Glass
Dianne Greene
Kelly Morgan Greenough
Elizabeth Gridley
Charlotte Guest
Nancy Gullatt
Hunter Johnson Haggart
Helen Jo Taylor Hardwick
Lea Ann Hardy
Jane Anne Harper
Marti Harris
Eva Hartig
Julie Haslam
Michelle Hassell
Carolyn Haught
Nan Hawkins
Meredith Hayes
Hayden Heinecke
Hope Heldmar
Diane Henderson
Scarlett Henley
Melanie Henry
Judy Herrmann
Kimberly Hicks
Sherrie Hicks
Shaunna Hjelm
Lurley Holt
Donna Hood
Stephanie Horne
Leslie Hoyt
Terri Huddleston
Deborah Smith Hughes
Kay Kirkpatrick Inhofe
Lana Istnick
Susie Jackson
Amy James
Candace M. Johnson
Deborah Austin Johnson
Nan Johnson
Jerri Jones
Sally White Jordan
Cheryl Kelsey
Marion Ryan Kelsey
Pat Kennedy

Susan M. Kirkpatrick
Deidra Kirtley
Brittany Kollmann
Amy Koontz
Kristen Kulling
Kitch Laenger
Ann H. Lake
Debbie Laughlin
Amy Lawson
Patty Lawson
Wendy M. Lea
Patricia Carroll Leikam
Casie Lewis
Lisa Linthicum
Nina Lipe
Sue Looney
Roxana Rozsa Lorton
JoAnne Lucas
DeEtta "Dee" Maguire
Wynne Marsh
Barbara Martin
Blake Martin
Leigh Martin
Pam Martin
Rita Martin
Sondra Martin
Robin McCullough
Gloria Grimes McFarland
Nikki McGooden
Lori McGraw
Margaret McShane
Melinda K. Mercer
Julie Meshri
Jennifer Miller
Nancy Tidwell Moore
Ginny Morehead
Pebble Moss
Lisa Muller
Janice P. Norris
Barb Bates Onyschuk
Melissa Perdue
Jacalyn Peter
Judith Peter
Stephanie Peters
Denise Piland
Deborah W. Pinkerton
Kathy Pixley
Sarah B. Powel
Donna Powell
Olene Presley
Ann Radford
Beth Rainey
Victoria Raley
Kathy Raschen
Sue Rauh

Catherine Reber
Bette Rector
Ann Reisch
Donna Rhyne
Heather Rhyne
Florine Richey
Melba Richey
Anne Richmond
Kelli Riddle
Tracy Rinehart
Janna Roberson
Celia Rosenberg
Michelle Rourke
Stephanie Royce
Marie Schlegel
Tracy Schloss
Mary Schmidt
Amy Schwier
E. Marie Scribner
Joan Seay
Jessica T. Selby
Tricia Shelton
Kim Smith
Lori Smith
Debbie Snellings
Lori Sonleiter
Sally Stewart
Mary Stoesser
Bryn Stratton
Susan Sullivan
Jean Tate
Lee Taylor
Amy Terry
Mitzi Thomas
Kathy Bogart Thompson
Susan McCalman Timo
Beverly Tolson
Kerry Turner
Heather Van Alstine
Valeria Vaughan
Kristin Vaughn
Renee E. Vause
Sharon Voskuhl
Beth Wagner
Marlo Wagner
Barbara Waple
Mary Warner
Jeannie Johnson West
Hope Wheeler
Eileene J. White
Fran M. Williams
Margaret B. Williams
Nancy M. Williams
Linda Wilson
Megan Zetik

INDEX

For more information or for additional copies of
Oil & Vinegar, please contact
The Junior League of Tulsa, Inc.
3633 South Yale
Tulsa, Oklahoma 74135
918-663-6100
www.jltulsa.org